IN THE BELLY
OF THE BEAST

IN THE BELLY OF THE BEAST

Letters from Prison

JACK HENRY ABBOTT

With an Introduction by Norman Mailer

Vintage Books
A Division of Random House, Inc.
New York

VINTAGE BOOKS EDITION, JANUARY 1991

Library of Congress Cataloging in Publication Data
Abbott, Jack Henry, 1944–
In the belly of the beast.
1. Abbott, Jack Henry, 1944–
2. Prisoners—United States—Biography.
3. Prisons—United States.
I. Title
HV9468.A22A37   1982   365'.44'0924 [B]   90-50214
ISBN 0-679-73237-3   AACR2

Manufactured in the United States of America
C9

ACKNOWLEDGMENTS

The preparation and arrangement of the letters in this book—fragmented letters to Norman Mailer—are the work of my editor at Random House, Erroll McDonald. I am grateful to him. My sister saw me through everything described in this book, and has kept something alive in me that would otherwise have perished long ago. I am grateful to her.

To Carl Panzram, William ("Whitey") Hurst, "Gypsy" Adams,
La Count Bly, Sam Melville, George Jackson,
"Curly" McFee, George ("Sugar Bear") Lovell, Gary Gilmore
—that they may rest in peace

INTRODUCTION

SOMETIME in the middle of working on *The Executioner's Song*, a note came from Morton Janklow, the literary agent. He was sending on a letter that had been addressed to him for forwarding to me. He assumed it was because our names had appeared together in a story in *People* magazine. In any event, the communication was by a convict named Jack H. Abbott, and Janklow felt there was something unusual in the fellow's letter. After I read it, I knew why he thought so.

An author will receive as many as several hundred letters a year from strangers. Usually they want something: will you read their work, or listen to a life-story and write it? This letter, on the contrary, offered instruction. Abbott had seen a newspaper account that stated I was doing a book on Gary Gilmore and violence in America. He wanted to warn me, Abbott said, that very few people knew much about violence in prisons. No author he had ever read on the subject seemed to have a clue. It was his belief that men who had been in prison as much as five years still knew next to nothing on the subject. It probably took a decade behind bars for any real perception on the matter to permeate your psychology and your flesh. If I were interested, he felt he could clarify some aspects of Gilmore's life as a convict.

There are unhappy paradoxes to being successful as a writer. For one thing, you don't have much opportunity to read good books (it's too demoralizing when you're at sea on your own work) and you also come to dread letter-writing. Perhaps ten times a year, a couple of days are lost catching up on mail, and there's little pleasure in it. You are spending time that could have been given to more dedicated writing, and there are so many letters to answer! Few writers encourage correspondents. My reply to a good, thoughtful, even generous communication from someone I do not know is often short and apologetic.

Abbott's letter, however, was intense, direct, unadorned, and detached—an unusual combination. So I took him up. When you got down to it, I did not know much about violence in prisons, and I told him so and offered to read carefully what he had to say.

A long letter came back. It was remarkable. I answered it, and another came. It was just as remarkable. I don't think two weeks went by before I was in the middle of a thoroughgoing correspondence. I felt all the awe one knows before a phenomenon. Abbott had his own voice. I had heard no other like it. At his best, when he knew exactly what he was writing about, he had an eye for the continuation of his thought that was like the line a racing-car driver takes around a turn. He wrote like a devil, which is to say (since none of us might recognize the truth if an angel told us) that he had a way of making you exclaim to yourself as you read, "Yes, he's right. My God, yes, it's true." Needless to say, what was true was also bottomless to contemplate. Reading Abbott's letters did not encourage sweet dreams. Hell was now clear to behold. It was Maximum Security in a large penitentiary.

Now, I was not the most innocent of tourists on trips into these quarters. I had, as I say, been working on *The Executioner's Song*, which apart from collateral reading in prison literature and trips to interview convicts and wardens had also provided me with Gilmore's letters to Nicole in the six months between his incarceration and his death. Those letters had their own penetration into the depths and horrors of prison life. Gilmore had his literary talents, and they were far from nonexistent. Still, he could not supply me with what Abbott offered. Gilmore, seen as a writer, rather than as a murderer, was a romantic and a mystic—ultimately, he saw incarceration as a species of karma. No matter how he might hate it, he also viewed it as the given. Life had its lights and shadows. Prison was the foul smell of the dark places, and maybe he had earned his sojourn there. That was the grim equation. Gilmore believed he would now find no happiness this side of death.

Out of Abbott's letters, however, came an intellectual, a radical, a potential leader, a man obsessed with a vision of more elevated human relations in a better world that revolution could forge. His mind, at its happiest, wanted to speak from his philosophical height across to yours. He was not interested in the particular, as Gilmore was, but only in the relevance of the particular to the abstract. Prison, whatever its nightmares, was not a dream whose roots would lead you to eternity, but an infernal machine of destruction, a design for the Dispose-All anus of a prodigiously diseased society.

The two men could not be more different. Gilmore, while always on the lookout to escape, still saw death as a species of romantic solution—he and Nicole could be together on the other side; Abbott, in contrast, might be ready by his convict's code to face death in any passing encounter, but he loathed death. It was the ultimate injustice, the final obscenity that society could visit on him.

Nonetheless, and it is one of those ironies that bemuses Abbott, he is the first to point out: ". . . if you went into any prison that held Gilmore and me and asked for all of the prisoners with certain backgrounds, both in and out of prison, backgrounds that include observed and suspected behavior, you will get a set of files, a list of names, and my file and name will always be handed you along with Gilmore's . . ."

Yes. Superficially, the morphology is close. Both were juvenile delinquents, both were incarcerated for most of their adolescence in state-supported institutions—as Abbott explained in his early letters, the kids you knew in the juvenile home were equal to relatives when you met them again in the pen—and both men knew very little of liberty. At thirty-six, Gilmore had spent eighteen of the last twenty-two years of his life in jail; and Abbott, while younger, had, proportionately, spent more. First imprisoned at twelve, he was out once for nine months, then imprisoned again at the age of eighteen for cashing a check with insufficient funds. He was given a maximum of five years. As he tells us in this work—it is no ordinary description of murder—he then killed a fellow convict and was given an indeterminate sentence up to nineteen years. He has been in jail ever since but for a six-week period when he escaped from Maximum Security in Utah State Prison and was on the lam in America and Canada. He has the high convict honors of being the only man to escape from Max in that penitentiary.

There are a few other similarities between Gilmore and Abbott. Foremost, they are both convicts. They are by their logic the elite of a prison population, part of the convict establishment as seen by the convicts, not by the authority—that is to say, they are hard-core. They see themselves as men who set the code for this city-state, this prison, that is occupied by a warden and his security officers. Beneath that overarching authority, convicts build their own establishment. They deal between themselves as contending forces, they hold trials, they instruct the young, they pass on the code.

There is a paradox at the core of penology, and from it derives the thousand ills and afflictions of the prison system. It is that not only the worst of the young are sent to prison, but the best—that is, the proudest, the bravest, the most daring, the most enterprising, and the most undefeated of the poor. There starts the horror. The fundamental premise of incarceration which Abbott demonstrates to us, over and over, is that prison is equipped to grind down criminals who are cowards into social submission, but can only break the spirit of brave men who are criminals, or anneal them until they are harder than the steel that encloses them. If you can conceive of a society (it is very difficult these days) that is more concerned with the creative potential of violent young men than with the threat they pose to the suburbs, then a few solutions for future prisons may be there. Somewhere between the French Foreign Legion and some prodigious extension of Outward Bound may lie the answer, at least for all those juvenile delinquents who are drawn to crime as a positive experience—because it is more exciting, more meaningful, more mysterious, more transcendental, more religious than any other experience they have known. For them, there is a conceivable dialogue. The authority can say: "Are you tough? Then show us you have the balls to climb that rock wall." Or travel down the rapids in a kayak, hang-glide—dare your death in any way that doesn't drag other people into death. Whereas for all those petty criminals who are not fundamentally attached to such existential tests of courage and violence, for whom crime is the wrong business, prison is not a problem. They can move with small friction from minimum security to prisons-without-walls to halfway houses. For them, a two-year sentence can even be a high-school education. But the social practice of mixing these two kinds of criminals together is a disaster, an explosion. The timid become punks and snitches, the brave turn cruel. For when bold and timid people are obliged to live together, courage turns to brutality and timidity to treachery. A marriage between a brave man and a fearful woman may be exceeded in matrimonial misery only by a union of a brave woman and a fearful man. Prison systems perpetuate such relations.

Abbott doesn't let us forget why. I cannot think, offhand, of any American writer who has detailed for us in equal ongoing analysis how prison is designed to gut and corrupt the timid, and break or brutalize the brave. No system of punishment that asks a brave human being to surrender his or her bravery can ever work for the common good. It violates the universal stuff of the soul out of which great civilizations are built.

We do not live, however, in a world that tries to solve its prison problems. Even to assume we do, is utopian. The underlying horror may be that we all inhabit the swollen tissues of a body politic that is drenched in bad conscience, so bad indeed that the laugh of the hyena reverberates from every TV set, and is in danger of becoming our true national anthem. We are all so guilty at the way we have allowed the world around us to become more ugly and tasteless every year that we surrender to terror and steep ourselves in it. The mugger becomes the

Golgotha and the middle class retires into walled cities
hed guards. Here, the prisons have wall-to-wall carpet-
the guards address the inmates as "Sir," and bow. But
they are prisons. The measure of the progressive imprisonment
of all society is to be found at the base—in the state of the
penitentiaries themselves. The bad conscience of society comes
to focus in the burning lens of the penitentiary. That is why
we do not speak of improving the prisons—which is to say,
taking them through some mighty transmogrifications—but
only of fortifying law and order. But that is no more feasible
than the dream of remission in the cancer patient. To read this
book is to live in the land of true and harsh perception—we
won't get law and order without a revolution in the prison
system.

Let me take it, however, from another tack. At one point in
these letters Abbott speaks of how he obtained his education
by reading books brought to him by his sister from a friendly
bookstore outside. For five and a half years in Maximum Security he read, with an intensity he has carried over into his style,
such authors as Niels Bohr and Hertz and Hegel, Russell and
Whitehead, Carnap and Quine. Crucial to it all was Marx. We
have the phenomenon of a juvenile delinquent brought up in
reform schools who stabs another prisoner to death, takes drugs
when he can, reads books in Maximum Security for five years
until he can hardly stand, and then, like Marx, tries to perceive
the world with his mind and come back with a comprehensive
vision of society. The boldness of the juvenile delinquent grows
into the audacity of the self-made intellectual. Only by the
tender retort of the heart can we imagine what it must be like
to live alone with so great a hunger and acquire the meat and
bones of culture without the soup. Abbott looks to understand
the world, he would dominate the world with his mind, yet in
all his adult life he has spent six weeks in the world. He knows
prison like the ferryman knows the crossing to Hades. But the
world Abbott knows only through books. He is the noble equivalent of Jerzy Kosinski's debased observer, Chauncey Gardner,
who learns about the world through a TV set. Yet, what a

prodigious meal Abbott has taken in. He has torn the meat of culture with his fingers, he has crushed the bones with his own teeth. So he has a mind like no other I have encountered. It speaks from the nineteenth century as clearly as from the twentieth. There are moments when the voice that enters your mind is the clear descendant of Marx and Lenin untouched by any intervention of history. Indeed, Abbott, who is half Irish and half Chinese, even bears a small but definite resemblance to Lenin, and the tone of Vladimir Ilyich Ulyanov rises out of some of these pages.

That offers a certainty. No one who reads this work will agree with every one of Abbott's ideas. It is impossible. On the one hand, he is the livid survivor of the ultra-revolutionary credo of the Declaration of Independence, *"life, liberty, and the pursuit of happiness."* Freedom and justice are oxygen to Abbott. He even writes: "It has been my experience that injustice is perhaps the *only* (if not merely the *greatest*) cause of insanity behind bars. You'd be surprised to learn what a little *old-fashioned* oppression can do to anyone." Hear! Hear! It is the devil's voice. We know it is true as soon as we hear it. Of course, Abbott is also a Communist. What kind, I'm not clear. He seems to hold to Mao, and to Stalin both, but vaguely. It is more clear that his real sympathies are with the Third World, with Cuba, Africa, and Arab revolutionaries. How long he would survive in a Communist country I don't know. It is obvious we would not agree on how long. We have written back and forth on this a little, but not a great deal. I no longer have the taste for polemic that he enjoys. Moreover, I have not spent my life in jail. I can afford the sophisticated despair of finding Russia altogether as abominable as America and more, but then, I have had the experience of meeting delegations of Russian bureaucrats and they look like prison guards in prison suits. I am free, so I can afford the perception. But if I had spent my young life in jail, and discovered the officers of my own land were my enemies, I would find it very hard not to believe that the officers of another land might be illumined by a higher philosophy.

I say this, and add that I am much more impressed by the literary measure of Abbott's writings on prison than by his overall analyses of foreign affairs and revolution. One is for me the meat and bones—the other is the soup he has not had. Yet I do not sneer. He has forged his revolutionary ideas out of the pain and damage done to his flesh and nerves by a life in prison. It is possible that he would be as much a revolutionary or more after ten years of freedom. Or an altogether different kind of man. I hope we have the opportunity to find out. As I am writing these words, it looks like Abbott will be released on parole this summer. It is certainly the time for him to get out. There is a point past which any prisoner can get nothing more from prison, not even the preservation of his will, and Abbott, I think, has reached these years. Whereas, if he gets out, we may yet have a new writer of the largest stature among us, for he has forged himself in a cauldron and still has half of the world to discover. There is never, when we speak of possible greatness in young writers, more than one chance in a hundred that we are right, but this one chance in Abbott is so vivid that it reaffirms the very idea of literature itself as a human expression that will survive all obstacles. I love Jack Abbott for surviving and for having learned to write as well as he does.

NORMAN MAILER
March 1981

CONTENTS

FOREWORD

CRITICIZING bourgeois economic laws based on the relationship between Robinsoe Crusoe and his servant Friday—laws still taught to schoolchildren as routinely as the story of Jesus Christ —Engels writes in *Anti-Dühring:*

Herr Dühring developed his argument in the field of morality and law. He started originally with one man, and he said: "One man conceived as being alone, or, what is in effect the same, out of all connection with other men, can have no *obligations;* for such a man there can be no question of what he *ought,* but only what he wants to do! But what is this man, conceived as being alone and without obligations, but the fateful, primordial Jew Adam in paradise, where he is without sin simply because there is no possibility for him to commit any?

". . .Adam is destined to fall into sin. Alongside this Adam there suddenly appears—not, it is true, an Eve with rippling tresses, but *a second Adam.* And instantly Adam acquires obligations and— breaks them. Instead of treating his brother as having equal rights and clasping him to his breast, he subjects him to his domination, he makes a slave of him."

Further on, Engels says: "All we can say is that we prefer the old Semetic tribal legend, according to which it is worthwhile for a man and a woman to abandon the state of innocence . . . and that to Herr Dühring will be left the uncontested glory of having constructed his original sin with two men." I.e., the original sin = social intercourse.

IN THE BELLY
OF THE BEAST

STATE-RAISED CONVICT

I'VE WANTED somehow to convey to you the sensations—the
atmospheric pressure, you might say—of what it is to be seriously a long-term prisoner in an American prison. That sentence does not adequately say what I mean. I've wanted to
convey to you what it means to be in prison after a childhood
spent in penal institutions. To be in prison so long, it's difficult
to remember exactly what you did to get there. So long, your
fantasies of the free world are no longer easily distinguishable
from what you "know" the free world is really like. So long,
that being free is exactly identical to a free man's dreams of
heaven. To die and go to the free world . . .

That part of me which wanders through my mind and never
sees or feels *actual* objects, but which lives in and moves
through my passions and my emotions, experiences this world
as a horrible nightmare. I'm talking now about the *me* in my
dreams. The one that appears in my dreams as me. The one
that is both the subject and object of all those surreal symbols.
The one that journeys within my life, within me, on what St.

John of the Cross viewed as a nighttime quest for fulfillment. When they talk of ghosts of the dead who wander in the night with things still undone in life, they approximate my subjective experience of this life.

. . .I have been desperate to escape for so many years now, it is routine for me to try to escape. My eyes, my brain seek out escape routes wherever I am sent, the way another prisoner's eyes, brain, seek friendliness, refuge or a warm, quiet place to rest and be safe. Too often for my liking those eyes and brains find me.

I escaped one time. In 1971 I was in the free world for six weeks. I was in a hotel room in Montreal, Canada. I was asleep. I had been a fugitive about three weeks. I began waking in the night in a sweat from bad dreams. I had simply been dreaming of prison. When I was *in* prison, I must have pushed all fear aside until not fearing was habitual. But that part of me I call my subjective side *did* feel that fear every minute of every day. Now the loathing and stark terror suppressed within me were coming to the surface in dreams. One morning I woke up and was plunged into psychological shock. I had *forgotten* I was free, I had escaped. I could not grasp where I was. I was in a nice bedroom with fancy furnishings. A window was open and the sunlight was shining in. There were no bars. The walls were papered in rich designs. My bed was large and comfortable. So much more. I must have sat there in bed reeling from shock and numbness for an hour while it all gradually came back to me that I had escaped.

So we can all hold up like good soldiers and harden ourselves in prison. But if you do that for too long, you lose yourself. Because there is something helpless and weak and innocent—something like an infant—deep inside us all that really suffers in ways we would never permit an insect to suffer.

That is how prison is tearing me up inside. It hurts every day. Every day takes me further from my life. And I am not even conscious of how my dissolution is coming about. Therefore, I cannot stop it.

I don't ever talk of these feelings. I never spent much time thinking of them. In fact, I'm only now thinking of them as I write this. I find it painful and angering to look in a mirror. When I walk past a glass window in the corridor and happen to see my reflection, I get angry on impulse. I feel shame and hatred at such times. When I'm forced by circumstances to be in a crowd of prisoners, it's all I can do to refrain from attack. I feel such hostility, such hatred, I can't help this anger. All these years I have felt it. Paranoid. I can control it. I never seek a confrontation. I have to intentionally gauge my voice in conversation to cover up the anger I feel, the chaos and pain just beneath the surface of what we commonly recognize as reality. Paranoia is an illness I contracted in institutions. It is not the reason for my sentences to reform school and prison. It is the effect, not the cause.

How would you like to be forced all the days of your life to sit beside a stinking, stupid wino every morning at breakfast? Or for some loud fool in his infinite ignorance to be at any moment able to say (slur) "Gimme a cigarette, man!" And I just look into his sleazy eyes and want to kill his ass there in front of God and everyone.

. . . Imagine a thousand more such daily intrusions in your life, every hour and minute of every day, and you can grasp the source of this paranoia, this anger that could consume me at any moment if I lost control.

LIES

It does not matter what is said and done
The eyes have it.
The mind's legislative faculty
Is unconcerned with appearances and words
Nothing is over and done with.
> Nothing.
Not even your malice.

Especially your malice.
So do not apologize to me.

I have walked stooped beneath your heart,
That cold-blooded crown
That holds the glinting jewel
Of contradiction in your eyes.

I think that I shall gouge them
From your skull
And crush them in my fist

—Give you a dog to see with
Give you eyes that pant and salivate,
Eyes that creep on all fours—
Eyes that cringe at the sound of my voice;
        Lie to me then.
Tell me life is good to you
—When all your memories are distilled
Into the transformed image, the Idea,
Of a mechanical hand reaching
To dig out your eyes.
        Lie to me then.
        Lie to me then, Dog-eyes.
        Lie to me then.

This is a poem I wrote in the arms of the prison muse
Paranoia here in the hole.

To be capable of writing something so mentally deranged—
to be able to write nothing else that expresses my social reaction to life—is very perplexing to me.

I wrote it this morning amid the infernal racket of a hundred
caged prisoners in single cells—racket of threats, race-talking
like there was no tomorrow.

I was born January 21, 1944, on a military base in Oscoda,
Michigan. I was in and out of foster homes almost from the

moment of my birth. My formal education: I never completed the sixth grade. At age nine I began serving long stints in juvenile detention quarters. At age twelve I was sent to the Utah State Industrial School for Boys. I was "paroled" once for about sixty days, then returned there. At age eighteen I was released as an adult. Five or six months later I was sent to the Utah State Penitentiary for the crime of "issuing a check against insufficient funds." I went in with an indeterminate sentence of up to five years. About three years later, having never been released, I killed one inmate and wounded another in a fight in the center hall. I was tried for the capital offense under the old convict statute that requires either *mandatory* death if malice *aforethought* is found, or a sentence of from three to twenty years. I received the latter sentence. An "indeterminate term" is what justifies the concept of *parole*. Your good behavior determines how long you stay in prison. The law merely sets a minimum and a maximum—the underlying assumption being that *no one* serves the maximum. A wrong assumption in my case. At age twenty-six I escaped for about six weeks.

I am at this moment thirty-seven years old. Since age twelve I have been free the sum total of nine and a half months. I have served many terms in solitary. In only three terms I have served over ten years there. I would estimate that I have served a good fourteen or fifteen years in solitary. The only serious crime I have ever committed in free society was bank robbery during the time I was a fugitive.

It was a big red-brick building with two wings. It stood about four stories high. It was constructed by the U.S. Army back when the state was still a territory. It was one of several buildings that had served as disciplinary barracks for the military. These barracks had long ago passed into the hands of the state and were part of a juvenile penal institution.

In the basement of the big red-brick building were rows of

solitary confinement cells. The basement was entered from outside the building only.

I am about twelve or thirteen years old. It is winter. I am marching in a long double-file of boys. We are marching to the mess hall. There is a guard watching as we march toward him. There is a guard walking behind us as we march.

My testes shrink and the blood is rushing and my eyes burn, ache. My heart is pounding and I am trying hard to breath slowly, to control myself.

I keep glancing at the guards: in front and behind the line.

The fields beyond are plowed and covered with an icy blanket of snow. I do not know how far beyond those fields my freedom lies.

Suddenly my confederate at the front of the line whirls and slugs the boy behind him. The front guard, like an attack dog, is on them both—beating them into submission. Seconds later the guard at the back rushes forward, brushing me as he passes.

I break away from the line, and run *for my life*. I stretch my legs as far as I can, and as quickly as I can, but the legs of a boy four feet six inches tall cannot stretch very far.

The fields are before me, a still flatland of ice and snow, and the huge clods of frozen, plowed earth are to me formidable obstacles. The sky is baby-blue, almost white. The air is clear.

I haven't covered fifty yards when I hear the pursuit begin: "You! Stop!" I immediately know I will be caught, but I continue to run.

I do not feel the blow of his fist. I'm in midair for a moment, and then I'm rolling in frozen clods of soil. I am pulled to my feet; one of my arms is twisted behind my back; my lungs are burning with the cold air; my nostrils are flared. I am already trying to steel myself for the punishment to come.

The other inmates stand in a long straight line, flanked by guards, and I am dragged past them. I do not respect them, because they will not run—will not try to escape. My legs are too short to keep up with the guard, who is effortlessly holding my arm twisted high up behind my back, so I stumble along, humiliated. I try hard to be dignified.

I see the door to the basement of the red-brick building, and we are approaching it in good time. A snowflake hits my eye and melts. It is beginning, softly, to snow.

At the top of the stairs to the basement, I am flung down against a high black-steel door. I stand beside it at attention as the guard takes out a huge ring of keys and bangs on the door. We are seen through a window. The door yawns open and an old guard appears, gazing at me maliciously.

We enter. We are standing at the top of a number of wide concrete steps that descend to the floor of the basement. I am thrown down the stairs, and I lie on the floor, waiting. My nose is bleeding and my ears are ringing from blows to my skull.

"Get up!"

Immediately I am knocked down again.

"Strip!"

I stand, shakily, and shed my clothing. His hands are pulling my hair, but I dare not move.

"Turn around!"

I turn.

"Bend over!"

I bend over. He inspects my anus and my private parts, and I watch, anxiously, hoping with all my might he does not hurt me there.

He orders me to follow him.

We enter a passageway between rows of heavy steel doors. The passage is narrow; it is only four or five feet wide and is dimly lighted. As soon as we enter, I can smell nervous sweat and feel body warmth in the air.

We stop at one of the doors. He unlocks it. I enter. Nothing is said. He closes and locks the door, and I can hear his steps as he walks down the dark passageway.

In the cell, there is a barred window with an ancient, heavy mesh-steel screen. It is level with the ground outside. The existing windowpanes are caked with decades of soil, and the screen prevents cleaning them. Through the broken ones I peer, running free again in my mind across the fields.

A sheet of thick plywood, on iron legs bolted to the floor,

is my bed. An old-fashioned toilet bowl is in the corner, beside a sink with cold running water. A dim light burns in a dull yellow glow behind the thick iron screening attached to the wall.

The walls are covered with names and dates—some of the dates go back twenty years. They were scratched into the wall. There are ragged hearts pierced with arrows and *pachuco* crosses everywhere. Everywhere are the words: "mom," "love," "god"—the walls sweat and are clammy and cold.

Because I am allowed only my undershorts, I move about to keep warm.

When my light was turned out at night, I would weep uncontrollably. Sixty days in solitary was a long, long time in those days for me.

When the guard's key would hit the lock on my door to signal the serving of a "meal," if I were not standing at attention in the far corner of the cell, facing it, the guard would attack me with a ring of keys on a heavy chain.

I was fed one-third of a regular meal three times a day. Only one day a week I was taken from my cell and ordered to shower while the guard stood in the shower-room doorway and timed me for three minutes.

Locked in our cells, we could not see one another, and if we were caught shouting cell-to-cell, we were beaten. We tapped out messages, but if they heard our taps, we were beaten—the entire row of cells, one child at a time.

I served five years in the big red-brick building, and altogether, two or three in solitary confinement. When I walked out, I was considered an adult, subject to adult laws.

I served so long because I could not adjust to the institution and tried to escape over twenty times. I had been there for the juvenile "crime" of "failure to adjust to foster homes."

. . .He who is state-raised—reared by the state from an early age after he is taken from what the state calls a "broken home" —learns over and over and all the days of his life that people in society can do anything to him and not be punished by the law. Do anything to him with the full force of the state behind them.

As a child, he must march in lock-step to his meals in a huge mess hall. He can own only three shirts and two pair of trousers and one pair of shoes.

People in society come to him through the state and injure him. Everyone in society he comes in contact with is in some capacity employed by the state. He learns to avoid people in society. He evades them at every step.

In *any* state in America someone who is state-raised can be shot down and killed like a dog by anyone, who has no "criminal record," with full impunity. I do not exaggerate this at all. It is a fact so ordinary in the minds of state-raised prisoners that it is a matter of common sense. If a prisoner were to show a skeptical attitude toward things of this nature, the rest of us would conclude that he is losing his mind. He is questioning what is self-evident to us: a practical fact of life.

. . .My mind keeps turning toward one of the main aspects of prison that separates ordinary prisoners who, at some point in their lives, serve a few years and get out never to return— or if they do, it is for another short period and never again— and the convict who is "state-raised," i.e., the prisoner who grows up from boyhood to manhood in penal institutions.

I have referred to it as a form of instability (mental, emotional, etc.). There is no doubt (let us say there is *little* doubt) that this instability is *caused* by a lifetime of incarceration. Long stretches of, say, from ages ten to seventeen or eighteen, and then from seventeen or eighteen to ages thirty and forty.

You hear a lot about "arrested adolescence" nowadays, and I believe this concept touches the nub of the instability in prisoners like myself.

Every society gives its men and women the prerogatives of men and women, of *adults*. Men are given their dues. After a certain age you are regarded as a man by society. You are referred to as "sir"; no one interferes in your affairs, slaps your hands or ignores you. Society is solicitous in general and serves you. You are shown respect. Gradually your judgment is tempered because gradually you see that it has real effects; it impinges on the society, the world. Your experience mellows your emotions because you are free to move about anywhere, work and play at anything. You can pursue any object of love, pleasure, danger, profit, etc. You are taught by the very terms of your social existence, by the objects that come and go from your intentions, the nature of your own emotions—and you learn about yourself, your tastes, your strengths and weaknesses. You, in other words, mature emotionally.

It is not so for the state-raised convict. As a boy in reform school, he is punished for being a little boy. In prison, he is punished for trying to be a man in the sense described above. He is treated as an adolescent in prison. Just as an adolescent is denied the keys to the family car for *any* disobedience, *any* mischief, I am subjected to the hole for *any* disobedience, *any* mischief. I will go to the hole for murder as well as for stealing a packet of sugar. I will get out of the hole in either case, and the length of time I serve for either offense is no different. My object is *solely* to avoid leaving evidence that will leave me open to prosecution out there in the world beyond these walls where a semblance of democracy is practiced.

Prison regimes have prisoners making extreme decisions regarding moderate questions, decisions that only fit the logical choice of either-or. No contradiction is allowed openly. You are not allowed to change. You are only allowed to submit; "agreement" does not exist (it implies equality). You are the rebellious adolescent who must obey and submit to the judgment of "grownups"—*"tyrants"* they are called when we speak of men.

A prisoner who is not state-raised tolerates the situation because of his social maturity prior to incarceration. He knows things are different outside prison. But the state-raised convict has no conception of any difference. He lacks experience and, hence, maturity. His judgment is untempered, rash; his emotions are impulsive, raw, unmellowed.

There are emotions—a whole spectrum of them—that I know of only through words, through reading and my immature imagination. I can *imagine* I feel those emotions (know, therefore, what they are), but *I do not*. At age thirty-seven I am barely a precocious child. My passions are those of a boy.

This thing I related above about emotions is the hidden, dark side of state-raised convicts. The foul underbelly everyone hides from everyone else. There is something else. It is the other half—which concerns *judgment, reason* (moral, ethical, cultural). It is the mantle of pride, integrity, honor. It is the high esteem we naturally have for violence, force. It is what makes us *effective*, men whose judgment impinges on others, on the world: Dangerous killers who act alone and *without* emotion, who act with calculation and principles, to avenge themselves, establish and defend their principles with acts of murder that usually evade prosecution by law: this is the state-raised convicts' conception of manhood, in the highest sense.

The model we emulate is a fanatically defiant and alienated individual who cannot imagine what forgiveness is, or mercy or tolerance, because he has no *experience* of such values. His emotions do not know what such values are, but he *imagines* them as so many "weaknesses" precisely because the unprincipled offender appears to escape punishment through such "weaknesses" on the part of society.

But if you behave like a man (a man such as yourself) you are doomed; you are feared and hated. You are "crazy" by the standards of the authorities—by their prejudices against prison-behavior.

Can you imagine how I feel—to be treated as a little boy and not as a man? And when I was a little boy, I was treated as a man—and can you imagine what that does to a boy? (I keep waiting for the years to give me a sense of humor, but so far that has evaded me completely.)

So. A guard frowns at me and says: "Why are you not at work?" Or: "Tuck in your shirttail!" Do this and do that. The way a little boy is spoken to. This is something I have had to deal with not for a year or two—nor even ten years—but for, so far, eighteen years. And when I explode, then I have burnt myself by behaving like a contrite and unruly little boy. So I have, in order to avoid that deeper humiliation, developed a method of reversing the whole situation—and I become the man chastising the little boy. (Poor kid!) It has cost me dearly, and not just in terms of years in prison or in the hole.

I cannot adjust to daily life in prison. For almost twenty years this has been true. I have never gone a month in prison without incurring disciplinary action for violating "rules." Not in all these years.

Does this mean I must die in prison? Does this mean I cannot "adjust" to society outside prison?

The government answers *yes*—but I *remember* society, and it is not like prison. I feel that if I ever did *adjust to prison*, I could by that alone never adjust to society. I would be back in prison within months.

Now, I care about myself and I cannot let it happen that I cannot adjust to freedom. Even if it means spending my life in prison—because to me prison is nothing but mutiny and revolt.

. . .A round peg will not fit into a square slot. I don't think they'll ever let me out of prison so long as my release depends upon my "good adjustment to prison."

In the beginning the walls of my cell were made of boiler-plate steel, and I would kick them all day every day, hollering, screaming—for no apparent reason. I was so choked with rage in those days (about sixteen or seventeen years ago), I could hardly talk, even when I was calm: I *stuttered* badly. I used to throw my tray as casually as you would toss a balled-up scrap of paper in a trash can—but would do it with a tray full of food at the face of a guard.

That is what I mean by a response to the prison experience by a man who does not belong there.

Hell, if I never went to prison, who knows what "evil" I would have committed. I'm not at all saying that because I don't *belong* in prison that I should not have been *sent* there. Theoretically, *no one* should *belong* in prison! I was sent there for punishment—and I happen to have gotten it. I do not think it is like that with most men who are sent to prison. Everyone hurts in prison, but not like that.

I *still* cannot talk to a guard, not unless I have his ass in a corner and am giving *him* the orders. I still stutter sometimes when I have to address a guard—address him without breaking rules. I can cuss one out very eloquently or insult him, but that's when I've broken a rule or don't care if I do break one. It is strange to contemplate: people with a stuttering defect in society can usually *sing* without stuttering; well, I can *cuss* without stuttering . . .

It's impossible. I'm the kind of fool who, facing Caesar and his starving lions, need only retract a statement to walk away scot-free but instead cannot suppress saying "fuck you" to Caesar—knowing full well the consequences. What is more, *I refuse to be martyred;* I don't accept the consequences, and whine all the way to my death. A death, it *seems*, that I *chose*.

If I *could* please Caesar, I would, I gladly would.

It's a fucked-up world, but it's all I got.

I have never accepted that I did this to myself. I have never been successfully indoctrinated with that belief. That is the only reason I have been in prison this long.

Indoctrination begins the moment someone is arrested. It

becomes more thorough every step of the way, from the moment of arrest to incarceration. In prison, it finds its most profound expression.

Every minute for years you are forced to believe that your suffering is a result of your "ill behavior," that it is self-inflicted. You are indoctrinated to blindly accept *anything* done to you. But if a guard knocks me to the floor, only by indoctrination can I be brought to believe I did it to myself. If I am thrown in the prison hole for having violated a prison rule—for having, for example, shown insolence to a pig—I can only believe I brought this upon myself through *indoctrination*.

. . .I might have become indoctrinated were it not for the evil and ignorant quality of the men who are employed in prisons.

A prisoner is taught that what is required of him is to *never* resist, *never* contradict. A prisoner is taught to *plead* with the pigs and accept guilt for things he never did.

I have had guards I have never seen before report me for making threats and arguing with them. I have been taken before disciplinary committees of guards for things I have never done, things they all knew I never did. And I have been ordered to the hole for things *they knew* I never did.

My prison record has in it more violence reported by guards than that of any of the 25,000 federal prisoners behind bars today, and I am not guilty of nine-tenths of the charges. Yet there is nothing at all I can do about it.

If I were beaten to death tomorrow, my record would go before the coroner's jury—before anyone who had the power to investigate—and my "past record of violence" would vindicate my murderers. In fact, the prison regime can commit any atrocity against me, and my "record" will acquit them.

The government shows that record to judges if I get into court on a civil suit against the prison or on a petition for writ of habeas corpus. It is designed to prejudice the judge—a man who relishes any opportunity to prejudice himself against prisoners.

. . .Responsibility? I am not responsible for what the government—its system of justice, its prisons—has done to me. I did not do this to myself.

This is not easy to say; it is not an easy *point of view* to hold. Why? Because it has cost me, so far, almost two decades of imprisonment. This I hold is the *greater* responsibility: I did not do this to myself.

I do not share in the sins of this guilty country; we are not "all in this together"! Who in America today would *dare* take the responsibility for himself and others that I and countless other prisoners like me have taken?

. . .I know you aren't mean enough to think I'm trying to shift the responsibility for my own "corrupt self." Indeed I am not. I have only tried to indicate the opposite: that I demand responsibility for myself. And in so doing, I have come to understand the reasons for it all. I myself can handle it quite well.

I do not have the confidence of a sleepwalker, and so my wish to better myself is in a spiritual sense a very conscious wish.

The Existentialists say they take all responsibility for their lives and the world upon their shoulders. Who can fault that? The world is amazed at how "cruel" it is! (This is very funny to think about!) And then, when the "chips are down" (Sartre's favorite expression), Sartre, who has never gambled but is enamored of the terminology of a kind of daring that doesn't involve getting his ass skinned, "martyrs" himself. It is the same kind of responsibility anyone takes upon himself by submitting to your bad opinion of him by hanging his head and agreeing with all the accusations—and then, when he has done that, forlornly tells you he is sorry it rained last night, sorry the price of tea went up, etc., etc. He won't defend himself, because he is *truly* at fault and is too pathetic to be punished.

To say you are *not* responsible for the life of someone you

killed in self-defense, not responsible for the circumstances
that brought you to prison (and kept you there for two decades)
—to say all that in the face of your accusers, accusers who also
justify their mistreatment of you by those accusations, is to be
really responsible for your words and deeds. Because every time
you reject the accusations, you are held responsible *further* for
things you are not responsible for.

. . .I've only lately discovered that at age thirty I began to
exercise the ability to *think*. I'm more restless now than I was
at age ten—and *nothing* could stop me then.

It is funny that some of us must not only get our bearings
but must also know all the details of the world before we
venture out into it. Only now do I feel I know enough to live,
but it is not funny that what I have learned may demand that
I throw that life away from me.

. . .I once served five and a half years in a cell in Maximum
Security, and for a period of over two years I did not speak to
anyone but my sister when she came to visit me twice a month.

When I entered Maximum Security, I was about five feet,
nine inches tall. I did not have a beard and did not know basic
arithmetic. When I emerged I could not walk without collaps-
ing; I had a full beard and was six feet tall. I had a rudimentary
understanding of mathematical theory and symbolic logic and
had studied in all the theoretical sciences. I had read all but
a very few of the world's classics, from prehistoric times up to
this day. My vision was perfect when I was locked up; when
I got out, my vision required glasses.

My good fortune resided in the fact that at that prison, a
prisoner was allowed to receive books directly from a bookstore
—so long as those books were not pornographic in any way.
(*Playboy* magazine was punishable contraband in prison then.)

Over the years, my sister had books sent to me from a single
bookstore, and the people who owned it searched out titles they

did not have in stock, free of extra charge, to send to me. That is where my education began. It has not ended to this day.

. . .There are not many books of philosophical importance I have not read. But knowledge comes from experience, and books only help understand experience. It has been not only my personal observation but the experience of all prison authorities: the most dangerous prisoners—and I mean that also in the "physical" sense—are "readers and writers."

In Maximum Security, I served *years* barefooted, with only my books and my balls and a punishment set of white standard (five sizes too large) coveralls. Novels and dictionaries. And then philosophy, until it came out of my eyes and ears—and finally, on occasion, my mouth: nine-tenths of my vocabulary I have never *heard* spoken. I remember the words "college" and "rhetoric." Small incidents of embarrassment when I discovered I had been pronouncing them wrong all my life. The word "guru" also—and "a priori." I fell into all the sciences at one time or another—so naïve in my grasp that I grasped things only someone like Bohr had. With me, I cannot learn practical things until I've studied the subject in the purest theoretical form. I did not really understand the first things about calculus until I studied Hertz and—of all people—Hegel on the subject. A child's primer would *mystify* me. Theoretical physics is simple to me, but applied physics leaves me stunned with a gross feeling. I can understand symbolic logic—Frege, Russell, Whitehead, Carnap, Quine, etc.—better then schoolboy arithmetic. It all found expression—and came together in the most elegant sense—in the findings of Marx. And that is a *world* of science and literature which the world you and I live in conceals from us. It took *great* effort and imagination on my part to seek out and obtain truly great advancements in our culture that the world we live in in the West tries so hard to suppress. Having contacted that world and communicated to a degree, to that degree I have become free.

Books are dangerous where there is injustice.

I've served time for just *requesting* books. I've been subjected to frame-ups and prejudice and the worst forms of discrimination because of the title of books I read. (Even a book with the word *Plato* on the cover can get you in trouble.)

No federal penitentiary (and there are only six top-level peniteniaries; the rest are ordinary prisons) has a prison library. The authorities say we "misuse" our knowledge if allowed to educate ourselves according to our natural impulses. They say we use the *Britannica* encyclopedias to make bombs, guns, acids, etc., etc., from the information they impart. They say Marx lies to us about our condition and makes us immoral and craven and desperate.

That is why they now have "education programs" in prison, i.e., so we learn *only* what they want us to learn. *I pride myself on the fact that I've never been in a prison school.*

You stumbled across the biggest sore-spot in the prison system when you asked why books are such touchy subjects to prison regimes. You have a problem understanding this because you are free and living in New York. But oppressed men know the value of books, because if they ever become enamored of, or even curious about, a *single* idea—and pursue it—they are on the road to rebellion. I mean by "rebellion" the bloodiest violence, the most ruthless murder and deterioration you can imagine. A taste of freedom in prison is not unlike a taste of heroin—a taste that obsesses you: a "taste" that addicts you—you'd *kill* for it in a literal sense. They go for your mind in prison today—where before, it was all physical suffering. The stakes are much, much greater today. The most dangerous convicts in American prison history are behind bars today. They kill quicker, more efficiently, are more liable to die for *beliefs*—more sophisticated in every way. I think you keep thinking of prison in terms of a military barracks. There is no comparison. It compares much more with a gladiator prison ("school") in ancient Rome during the suppression of slaves and Christians. We are naturally pitted against each other by degrees of stoicism (a kind of "class" system) through prison manipulation.

The *books* we have we hold almost by force of arms—
literally. We have no legal rights *as prisoners*, only as citizens.
The only "rights" we have are those left to their "discretion."
So we assert our rights the only way we can. It is a compromise,
and in the end I greatly fear we as prisoners will lose—but the
loss will be society's loss. We are only a few steps removed from
society. After us, comes you.

Yes, it is frightening, but more frightening to me is the plain
fact that society has dropped its guard and placed too much
trust in government.

That is why I write you. Because I am very concerned about
these matters.

. . .I will continue striving to learn to write. But it is like
learning to swim on land. I'll learn as much as I can. It is
difficult for me to take it seriously or to feel comfortable about
it. It is as if I were sitting in an audience listening to fine
gentlemen and scholars deliver speeches and discourses on
things of reverence to me. Then one of them suddenly looks
across the numberless audience directly at me and says: "It's
your turn, Jack. Come up here and say something."

It isn't difficult to imagine my embarrassment—and my
delight: two emotions that create a kind of mixed confusion I
do not know the word for. Gratitude is close.

As I said, I'll try.

. . .*I am not an intellectual, because my thoughts are primarily
to me a predicate to action.*

I told you long ago that I know no other way. No one, not
even you (but you have come the closest, and that in itself is
a pathetic fact), has ever held out a hand to help me to be a
better man. No one. I am doing my best on my own and with
what I have to work with, which is meager.

I told you at the beginning I was, you might say, not likable
at all. I never tried to prettify anything. I never tried to appeal
to you.

I've never kept a diary, but the closest I came was my letters to you. My life is not a "saga" and I resent your using the term like that. I do not feel "heroic." But I am caught in an experience of life not the subject of common dissertation. You expressed an interest in it. I meant to accommodate that interest to the fullest of my abilities.

I never preached to you, nor tried to convert you. My respect would not allow that. Besides, I know more than most the futility of debate in such matters.

VARIETIES
OF PUNISHMENT

ALL TORTURE aims at taking things out of you by force.
No one has the right to take Jack Abbott away from Jack
Abbott. Not my soul. Yet that is what is being done to me.
I have become a stranger to my needs and desires. And
without meaning to sound conceited or to brag, I can honestly say I cannot imagine anyone with more moral stamina,
more psychological endurance and more will power than I
myself have. I have measured these things and I know. I
have seen men around me through the years fall apart morally, seen them go mad in subtle ways and seen them surrender their will to the routine of prison, and I have
resisted it all much, much longer than others. So it is not
that I am "weak" in those areas, but rather it demonstrates
the immensity of the power, the greatness of the forces
that are brought to bear to change men, even though *no
one* (not the wardens or the pigs or the government) can
control that power, that force, in such a way as to change a

man to become what we consider a fair version of
"Rehabilitated Man," i.e., the good citizen.

. . .A great number of practices in prisons these last fifteen
to twenty years have been *legally* abolished as cruel and unbe-
coming to these "civilized times" it is alleged that we live
in.

Some of us prisoners—not many; there are only a few of us
left who have *never* been free—are a *product* of prison conditions that are today recognized as "unconstitutional," indeed,
criminal.

What are we supposed to do? No one has yet apologized to
us. The same pigs—or their stripe—still preside over these
prisons. Do they "like" me? You would think so; none of them
wants ever to see me free again.

This is part of the indoctrination. I am supposed to be *glad*
they abolished methodical torture instruments in prison! Glad
they "abolished" horsewhipping, corporeal punishment, starvation.

But even if I *did* feel "appreciation," what good would it do
me? I have long ago been taken light-years away from any
ameliorating effect which punishment that aims at rehabilitation can possibly achieve.

It is called *affirmative action.* It is applied by the government
to develop programs and policies aimed at correcting past injustices suffered by minorities in our society.

I can easily understand the justice of this doctrine—but the
government will not apply it to men like me, even though it
is completely understood that I survived prison conditions
which are illegal and have never once from that time to this
been given a chance to walk free from prison.

I have gained a *reputation* among prison authorities that
extends from the time those illegal conditions existed, that

stretches to this very day unbroken. I simply resisted those
conditions that today are "officially" abolished—but at the
time, the law was not on my side. Any more than it is today.

. . .My first acquaintance with punitive long-term solitary
confinement had a more adverse and profound spiritual effect
on me than anything else in my childhood.

I suffered from *claustrophobia* for years when I first went to
prison. I never knew any form of suffering more horrible in my
life.

The air in your cell vanishes. You are smothering. Your eyes
bulge out; you clutch at your throat; you scream like a banshee.
Your arms flail the air in your cell. You reel about the cell,
falling.

Then you suffer cramps. The walls press you from all directions with an invisible force. You struggle to push it back. The
oxygen makes you giddy with anxiety. You become hollow and
empty. There is a vacuum in the pit of your stomach. You
retch.

You are dying. Dying a hard death. One that lingers and toys
with you.

The faces of guards, angry, are at the gate of your cell.
The gate slides open. The guards attack you. On top of all
that, the guards come into your cell and beat you to the
floor.

Your mattress is thrown out. Your bedsheets are doubled.
One end is run through a hole under the steel bunk that hangs
from your cell wall. The other end is pulled through a hole at
the opposite end of your bunk.

Your ankles are handcuffed and so are your hands. The sheet
runs through them and you are left hanging from a spit by your
feet and your hands. Your back is suspended several inches
above the floor. You are smothering. You are being crushed to
death.

They leave you like that all night.

That is how, over and over again, I was "cured" of the

malady called claustrophobia. It took at least three or four years.

I was twenty or twenty-one years old when I was taken from the prison to an old county jail where I was to be booked and tried for killing another prisoner in combat.

I tried to escape from the jail. The jailers reopened a cell that had not been used in twenty-five years and placed me in it under prison discipline—a starvation diet of a bowl of broth and a hard biscuit once a day. It was a *blackout cell*. I was given a canvas sleeping mat and the door was closed on me. There was an iron sink-and-toilet combined in the corner, and other than that, there was nothing except about two inches of dust on the floor.

It was in *total* darkness. Not a crack of light entered that cell *anywhere*—and I searched, in the days that followed, for such a crack along every inch of the door and the walls. The darkness was so absolute it was like being in ink.

There was an ingenious apparatus on the door. It was cylindrical and was hand-operated from outside the cell. The jailer would place the bowl and the biscuit on a platform in the cylindrical apparatus. Then he would bang the door twice with his keys and I could hear the mechanism creak. I would crawl to the door, feeling my way up to the apparatus. When my hands came into contact with the food, I would carefully take it out and consume it. Then I would return the bowl to the platform in the apparatus and he would revolve it so that it returned to him outside the door.

In this entire process, I was fed without a glimmer of light. Darkness muffles sound. The only sound I ever heard—outside of my own movements and mutterings—was the bang of the keys and the creaking of the apparatus once a day.

The only light I saw was when I closed my eyes. Then there was before me a vivid burst of brilliance, of color, like fireworks. When I opened my eyes it would vanish.

It is one thing to *volunteer* for an experiment and intentionally consent to be plunged into darkness like this. It is another thing for it to be forced on you, for light to be *taken* from you.

My eyes *hungered* for light, for color, the way someone's dry mouth may *hunger* for saliva. They became so sensitive if I touched them; they exploded in light, in showers of white sparks shooting as if from a fountain.

Whenever I stirred in the cell, dust rose to my nostrils. Insects crawled on me when I was lying down and I became a ball of tension.

I counted twenty-three days by the meals. Then once I rose, thirsty, and felt my way to the sink. I felt the cup and I grasped it in my right hand. I closed my eyes for a moment and a shower of red and blue rained on me. I opened them to midnight darkness. With my left hand I felt for the button on the sink. I pressed it and could hear the trickle of water. I held my cup under it until I judged it full. Then I raised the cup carefully to my lips and tilted it back to drink.

I felt the legs, the bodies of many insects run up my face, over my eyes and into my hair. I flung down the cup and brought my hands to my face in an electric reaction and my eyes closed and the fireworks went off again.

I heard someone screaming far away and it was me. I fell against the wall, and as if it were a catapult, was hurled across the cell to the opposite wall. Back and forth I reeled, from the door to the walls, screaming. Insane.

When I regained consciousness, I was in a regular cell. I had been removed from the *blackout cell*. Every inch of my body was black with filth and my hair was completely matted.

I do not think *blackout cells* are in use in many prisons and jails today . . .

. . .They *are* still in use today and they are *not* used for "medical reasons." They are used for punishment. They are called *strip-cells* and I have been thrown in strip-cells many times—sometimes for months on end. This is prison *justice*.

There is no facility for running water in such a cell. The

diabolic minds that design these punishment cells chill me when I consider them. The idea behind this one is that a prisoner in a strip-cell must "request" *water* from a guard. I don't think it would tax your imagination to see that a prisoner is reduced to *begging for water*.

It is a big square concrete box. The cell has nothing on the walls except for a single solid-steel door at the entrance. The ceiling is vaulted about fifteen feet above the floor and there is a bare lightbulb that stays lit, day and night.

In fact, there is no way to discern the days in the cell except by counting the times you are served your food through a slot in the door. How do you connect this with what you have done to be placed there?

The floor inclines from the walls inward to the center of the cell. It inclines gradually, like the bottom of a sink. A toilet bowl is more accurate. Then, in the center of the floor, there is a *hole* about two inches in diameter. It is flush with the concrete floor—as flush as a hole on a golf course. At first its purpose mystifies you.

Stains of urine and fecal matter radiate outward from the hole to within a foot or so from the walls. The stench is ever-present.

There is no bed-rack or bunk. There is nothing but the smell of shit and piss, and the glare of the light—out of reach— which is never extinguished.

The light is present even when you close your eyes. It penetrates the eyelids and enters your visual sensations in a grayish-white glow, so that you cannot rest your eyes. It *throbs* always in your mind.

Usually you are given nothing to wear but a pair of undershorts, and if you are lucky, you will receive a sleeping mat and a bedsheet.

At first you move gingerly about the cell because of the body wastes of prisoners who preceded you. You spend much of your time in the first long days squatting with your back defensively against a wall—squatting on the outskirts of the filth on the floor which radiates from the hole. Staring into it. If it were desolation you were facing as you stare off in your cell, it would probably inspire you in some small way. Poets have sung songs of scenes of desolation.

But what faces you is a cesspool world of murk and slime; a subterranean world of things that squirm and slide through noxious sewage, piles of shit and vomit and piss. There is the smell of unwashed feet and nervous sweat of bodies foreign to yours, so closing your eyes gives no relief.

If you are in that cell for weeks that add up to months, you do not ignore all this and live "with it"; you *enter* it and become a part of it.

I never suffered from thirst. No one there does, really. There is enough moisture in the food to hold that back. But I have been so dry in the mouth that I could not swallow, I could not talk, for weeks. You "ask" for water like this: "Wa? Wa?"

This is the strip-cell. Not only do these cells still exist in every state in this country, even the architects of modern prison facilities include them in new institutions.

Any sane man may wonder: What grievous crime would a man have to commit to be thus treated? The answer: In prison, anything at all. Any indiscretion. A contraband book. A murder. A purloined sandwich. This does not even square with the savage's conception of justice: *An eye for an eye.*

. . .There was once a form of prison discipline called *the starvation diet.* You were thrown in the hole and fed once a day just barely enough to give you the minimum nourishment to exist: to exist *in the hole,* not to exist the way the average man does.

This was still being done only ten years ago. Some places gave you bread and water once a day—but the maximum calculated by that strange brand of physicians I can think of only as technicians of pain was *ten days* of this. Then you came off for at least twenty-four hours of regular three meals served you over that twenty-four-hour period. Then you were placed *back* on another ten-day stint of starvation—that is, if you had misbehaved *in the hole*. Otherwise, after ten days you were let out of the hole.

All told, I served, in three years, the sum of *one year on the starvation diet*. That was when I first entered prison as a child of eighteen.

The longest stretch I ever pulled was about seventy *consecutive* days.

At this prison, the maximum you could obtain in a sentence to the hole under starvation conditions was *twenty-nine days*. Usually the sentence never exceeded fourteen days—or two weeks. That was for an average *misdemeanor*, a minor infraction of rules.

I went there once for spitting back at a pig who had spit in my face. My sentences were *always* the most severe, and so I was taken there under a twenty-nine-day sanction by the captain's committee.

State custom permitted us these items when we were living under starvation conditions in the hole:

1) one Christian Bible or one *Book of Mormon*. No other reading matter or religious matter allowed;

2) one set of white coveralls made of white canvas material (the gun-tower guards had orders to shoot anyone they saw on the yard in this disciplinary garb; it identified you the way a shaved head identified kids at the Industrial School for Boys who were rebellious);

3) one sleeping mat and a bedsheet.

Nothing more. You could receive neither your mail nor *any* visits. This included legal mail from the courts as well as mail from your lawyer—no lawyer could even visit you during this period of discipline. When your time was over, you were handed your back mail in a heap.

I had been there for about two weeks, and one evening, just as the guard was exiting after making his rounds to count us, someone shouted: "Fuck you!"

The pig called down the range: "Okay, Abbott! That's another report!" Then he left.

The inmate volunteered to confess he did it to save me from

more time on starvation. In those days prisoners backed each other, and an injury to one was an injury to us all. I cited this code and told him I had to ride it out.

The next day the guards escorted me to the captain's disciplinary committee and I was sentenced to another twenty-nine-day stint, to be served after the one I was then halfway through.

A little later on, I soaked my Bible in the toilet and wrapped it tightly with strips of cloth from my bedsheet to form a hefty bludgeon. This was done because the day before, I had been rousted by pigs who pretended they were searching my cell and beaten up in the process. When the guard came by the next day, I lured him up to the bars of my cell and hit him with it, making a gash across his forehead.

When I was taken before the captain's committee, I was given another twenty-nine-day stint back-to-back with the other two sanctions. He passed the slip of paper the order was written on across the table to me and I picked it up, wadded it carefully into a ball and bounced it off his chest.

I was given yet another twenty-nine-day sanction. That made four of them I had to do—roughly *four months.*

After my *first* stint was over, I was not taken off for three meals (twenty-four hours). I caused a ruckus and received another twenty-nine-day sanction and then, finally, another.

A total of *six months.* It was, in fact, the death penalty. I was going to die if I remained on the starvation diet that long *for sure.* Every prisoner and guard knew this. The inmate who shouted "Fuck you" to the pig was out of the hole and on the yard, but he went to the captain and told him it was *he* who shouted the obscenity at the guard and not I, in an effort to save me. It did no good.

. . .Have you ever experienced *forced* starvation? It is not even *close* to a diet or a fast. Those things are *voluntarily* entertained.

When the gate slides closed behind you in that cell in which you are going to be subjected to methodical starvation, you face the fact that you have to survive the worst periods of it—the last days before it is over. You have to preserve yourself, so you cannot pace your cell; in fact, you must keep every motion you make down to a necessary minimum. You do the sanction lying in your bunk.

Most convicts, then, when they entered these starvation conditions, always gave their first once-a-day to the man who had been there the longest and needed it more. Likewise, his last day he gives his once-a-day to the one who needed it more. The greater need was calculated by days and was mechanical.

You suffer psychologically at first, That is why overweight men complained more. But when it gets down to physical survival, the suffering is real.

I learned a little secret in this period. A convict over sixty years old passed it on to me: cockroaches are a source of protein. Mash the day's catch all together in a piece of bread and swallow it like a big pill. I went beyond this, and before it was over, included every bug I could catch. It gives you a weird glow and feels strange to your metabolism when you begin to starve.

You may have one bowel movement but never more then two under starvation conditions. Your stomach shrinks up into a tight ball. This is what causes *hunger pangs*. When it has shrunken completely, the hunger pangs are no more. You are no longer hungry, although the rest of your body begins to take over the pain and extend it. Your limbs express hunger when your muscle tissue begins to dissolve. It is a strange kind of pain to feel. The need to eat becomes a need to devour, like an animal.

If you bloat yourself on water, you only prolong the pain in your stomach and it will multiply the other expressions of suffering starvation.

I once caught myself considering the arm of a pig, and became excited the way, I guess, a carnivorous beast becomes excited to see his dinner on the hoof. It was as if I could smell his blood.

I had completed sixty days when there was an inmate work strike. The pigs filled the hole to maximum capacity with strikers. I was no longer suffering stomach hunger pangs and my muscles were all but dissolved by then. I had again not been given my twenty-four-hour respite.

I recall I just quit consuming my once-a-day and gave it to the strikers in solidarity. I insisted on it and even threw it out of my cell when they refused to accept it from me. I had entered indifference, almost euphoria. Yet, they say I roamed the floor, picking. Looking, I imagine, for my bugs. All I recall is one day I saw the gate to my cell open in a slow drowsy haze. I had heard shouting and scuffling vaguely all that day. The prisoners tried to take a hostage to demand my release from starvation. I found all this out later.

I could barely make out the few blurred faces bobbing toward me as I lay in my bunk. One of them carried me in his arms to the infirmary. I have flashes of memory of being carried up the main corridor.

About a week later I awoke in a hospital cell with a tube down my nasal passage to my stomach and there was a bottle of clear liquid suspended upside down with a tube attached that ran into my arm.

When they couldn't handle you in segregation or the Grade (Maximum Security confinement)—and you had to be way-out —you were thrown in a special cell on the third floor of C Cellhouse (in the *office* of death row—the old death row): one cell called "C-300." It was a cube of boiler-plate steel with a solid-steel door. It was the "gas tank"—where you were tear-gassed and there was no ventilation. There, they once did not feed me for a week. They gave me only a glass of water a day. I was kept chained to the floor for periods of one to two weeks. "Normally," I was unchained. Once I was kept there a year. I did a six-month stretch there another time.

I was in that cell the day J. F. Kennedy was assassinated (death row was cheering; they had heard it on the news).

I was there the day a pig with a wooden leg (a pig who used to spit in my face when the outer steel door was opened)

opened the outer door and declared: *"Your mother died last night!"*—and then he slammed the door in my face. This is how I learned of her death.

No one has ever done the time I did in C-300. Nor has anyone served as long as five years—from January 1966 to March 1971—in Maximum Security as I have. I had to escape to get out.

. . .I am on the Grade. I am pacing my cell after the evening meal. I hear a voice whispering loudly through the ventilator on the back wall of my cell. It is saying "I'm gonna kill you! You son-of-a-bitch!" It is saying "Jack! Jack Abbott! You are going to die!" There is a string of obscenities. No one can hear this except me.

I go to the vent in quick rage: "Who is it!?" There is silence for a moment, then: "Fuck you! It's me, Abbott! It's me!"

I'm thinking it is the prisoner in the cell on the tier opposite mine, on the other side of the plumbing pipe-run. I call him by name. He comes to *his* vent. He tells me he doesn't know what I'm talking about. He withdraws.

The voice returns. I peer carefully through a crack in the ventilator. I see a hand move. It is a pig.

I shout at him and he *whispers* loudly back to me—threats and obscenities. I shout that I'm going to get even. He leaves.

No other prisoner heard him. I tell them what the pig did to me. He has to make his rounds to count. When he comes by, I will throw a cup of water on him.

He comes by—grinning evilly at me. I douse him.

The trap slams closed.

My cell door slides open. Guards pour onto the tier. We fight; they leave. They had been waiting for me to throw the water.

The next day I am taken before the captain's committee and given a twenty-nine-day sentence to the hole on starvation diet.

I tell the captain the pig had been threatening me and calling me names through my ventilator.

A psychiatrist sees me in the hole. He tells me I am hal-
lucinating. I am placed on injections of two hundred milli-
grams of Thorazine three times a day.

At that time I was barely nineteen years old. I was one of
the first prisoners in this country subjected to drug therapy in
prison. Now it is common.

I fought every time, until I could fight no more. (Five or six
guards entered the cell and wrestled me to the floor three times
a day and injected Thorazine into me.) I suffered severe physical side effects. At that time, there was not much known about
the side effect called the "Parkinson's reaction." The prison
doctor thought I was feigning.

This gave me my first psychiatric record.

. . .This letter is about the instability "crazies" have in
prison. It is about how we who suffer from this prison-cul-
tivated disease are dealt with.

X told me he once saw Gilmore transfixed, frozen on the
nerve-endings of his central nervous system. You do not always
die any more from crucifixion; the authorities try not to let that
happen. I've myself been crucified a hundred times and more
by those institutional drugs that are for some sinister reason
called "tranquilizers."

They are *phenothiazine* drugs, and include Mellaril, Thorazine, Stelazine, Haldol.

Prolixin is the worst I've ever experienced. One injection
lasts for two weeks. Every two weeks you receive an injection.
These drugs, in this family, do not calm or sedate the nerves.
They attack. They attack from so deep inside you, you cannot
locate the source of the pain. The drugs *turn* your nerves in
upon yourself. Against your will, your resistance, your resolve
are directed at your own tissues, your own muscles, reflexes, etc.
These drugs are designed to render you so totally involved with
yourself physically that all you can do is concentrate your entire
being on holding yourself together. (Tying your shoes, for
example.) You cannot cease trembling.

From all of these drugs you can get the "Parkinson's reaction"—a physical reaction identical to Parkinson's disease. The muscles of your jawbone go berserk, so that you bite the inside of your mouth and your jaw locks and the pain throbs. For *hours* every day this will occur. Your spinal column stiffens so that you can hardly move your head or your neck and sometimes your back bends backward like a bow and you cannot stand up.

The pain *grinds* into your *fiber;* your vision is so blurred you cannot read. You ache with restlessness, so that you feel you have to walk, to pace. And then as soon as you start pacing, the opposite occurs to you: you must *sit* and *rest*. Back and forth, up and down you go in pain you cannot locate; in such wretched anxiety you are overwhelmed, because you cannot get relief even in *breathing*. Sometimes a groan or whimper rises inside you to the point it comes out involuntarily and people look at you curiously, so you suppress the noise as if it were a belch—this sound that is wrung out of your soul.

You can see it. We walk stiff-backed and we don't swing our arms as we walk . . .

We are not crazy, so why do they do it? Because they fear us; we are dangerous. We fear nothing they can do to us, not even the drugs, the crucifixion.

No doubt there are those who need these drugs; do not get me wrong. I do not pretend to be a doctor. Those who need the drugs, who are ill, do *not* experience it the way we do. They know this, the prison regime knows this little trick.

It is like electroshock treatment: there are those who benefit by it. But administer this to a man who is healthy and does not require it for medical reasons and it becomes a form of torture. It is painful, a nightmare. Fifteen years ago it was used to punish prisoners.

When the captain and the pigs cannot discipline you, cannot intimidate and therefore hurt and punish you, *control* you, you are handed over to a "psychiatrist," who doesn't even look at you and who orders you placed on one of these drugs. You see, there is something wrong with your mind if you defy the

worst "official" punishment a prison regime can legally dish up.
That is their logic.

For *years* they have put me through this cycle over and over
again: captain-doctor-broken-rule. Over and over. A pig pushes
me, I *instinctively* push back, sometimes slug him. That starts
it. Eventually I end up stammering like an idiot and staggering
about—usually for six months to a year at a time—on the
drugs, until finally I'm taken off the drugs and turned loose
with the "normal" prisoners in the main prison population. I
go along there until the next "incident" that leads to my
"discipline," and once more the cycle begins, like a crazy
carousel, a big "merry-go-round."

They know what they are doing, even if they never admit
it to anyone. They will not even admit it to *me*. No one expects
me to become a better man in prison. So why not say it: The
purpose is to ruin me, ruin me completely. The purpose is to
mark me, to stamp across my face the mark of this beast they
call prison.

. . .I write with my blood because I have nothing else—and
because these things are excessively painful to recall. It drains
me.

. . .There is a saying: *The first cut is the deepest.* Do not
believe that. The first cut is nothing. You can spit in my face
once or twice and it is nothing. You can take something away
that belongs to me and I can learn to live without it.

But you cannot spit in my face every day for ten thousand
days; you cannot take all that belongs to me, one thing at a
time, until you have gotten down to reaching for my eyes, my
voice, my hands, my heart. You cannot do this and say it is
nothing.

I have been made oversensitive—my very *flesh* has been
made to suffer sensations and longings I never had before. I
have been chopped to pieces by a life of deprivation of sensations; by beatings so frequent I am now a piece of meat and
bone; by lies and by drugs that attack my nervous system. I
have had my mind turned into steel by the endless smelter of
time in confinement.

I have been twisted by justice the way other men can be twisted by love . . .

Once I was taken from the Atlanta Federal Penitentiary to the Butner, North Carolina, Federal Correctional Institution for psychological experimentation—the result of being falsely accused of involvement in an almost-fatal knife assault on a prison guard.

At Butner, I was told almost immediately upon my arrival that an unnamed informer among the inmates had reported that I was planning to escape.

I was taken by about twenty guards and other employees into a special psychological observation cell. Butner was built from the ground up with architectural concepts almost futuristic in design. It is extremely modern and could easily be a set for a space-age movie.

The psychological observation cell I was taken into was designed like a fish tank (an aquarium)—except, of course, the glass was unbreakable. It is impossible to see or hear another human being, or to be seen or heard by anyone but the prison staff.

The floor was concrete and in the center was a drain, with a round grating over it, such as in a shower stall.

One steel slab sat on iron legs bolted to the floor. This was the "bed," and there was nothing else in the cell. There was a rubber mat on it about an inch thick.

I was stripped nude. I was forced to lie on the steel slab. Each of my ankles was chained to a corner of the bed-structure, and my wrists were chained over my head to the other two corners, so I was chained down in a complete spread-eagle position.

There were a few females on the staff (most were also U.S. Army personnel). This was in 1976—the latter part.

In order to urinate I had to twist my torso so that my penis would hang in a general direction over the side of the bed-structure, and the urine would cross the floor and go down the drain I described above.

I was hand-fed at each meal.

The day after I was chained down, several guards entered the cell and beat me with their fists all over my face, chest and stomach. I was choked manually and brought to the point—almost—of strangulation, and then they would remove their hands. My throat was blue with bruises caused this way.

I was chained—now I mean *iron* chains, not "leather restraints"—in this manner for ten days, and I was attacked three times in this period.

Finally the "medical technician" observed that the nerves in my arms were dying—the areas between wrists and elbows.

So about twenty guards came again. They unchained me and dressed me in nylon coveralls. As I was dressing I glanced in the window at my reflection and my face was black and both eyes swollen. I was covered with bruises.

They put me in handcuffs and leg-irons and took me to the regular segregation section. There only one of my hands was kept chained to the iron crossbar at the head of the bed. I could stand. It was at that time that I began writing *you*, in the hole, with one hand chained to my bed.

I was kept chained by one hand until I was rushed to the federal medical center in Missouri. My gall bladder was removed. I had gallstones, but the beatings had agitated the condition, and I learned that the tissue of my gall bladder had broken due to the jolts of the stones pressed against the organ.

. . .The guards form a loose gauntlet from your cell to the shower stall. You must cross the floor, a distance of about thirty yards. They look at you as if you are not there, but are alert to every move you make. They register your facial expression to see if you are anything but meek, *humble.* Anything else raises their hackles, and their mouths turn down at the corners and they ball up their hands into fists at their sides.

You are nude. The floor is wet from the prisoners before you who trailed it from the showers. There are also spots of blood, fresh.

You stare at the floor. You must slump your shoulders and drag your feet when you take steps. You must go slowly—but not too slowly. Your gait must be timid. You must not slip on the floor.

Fold your arms. Fold your arms behind your back. That is the best way to assure them you are incapable of harm. It is one of the postures of the meekly insane. Try to make them laugh at you. Cringe; that should do it.

Do not tell me you would not follow these instructions. You will be pounded to the floor otherwise. The guards are hired by the pound. They are Missouri rednecks from the Ozark regions. Alone with one or two, they are profoundly afraid of anyone. But six or seven are afraid of nothing one prisoner, naked, can do. It does not matter the least how strong or dangerous the prisoner is. Not there it doesn't.

Everything is framed by a soft blur that radiates outward into a vague fog. Your mind is not working any longer. You have no questions, either for yourself or others. This is because you are under the influence of a phenothiazene drug—any one (or combination) of ten or fifteen such drugs known by the brand names. Mixed with terrorism, it equals living death.

They all accomplish the same, but each has its little idiosyncrasy. If you have been on regular dosages of Mellaril, your testicles will not produce sperm. If you masturbate—if you can somehow manage to accomplish a fantasy erection—you will experience at orgasm every sensation of tension and ejaculation you should experience, but with this difference: absolutely no substance issues from the ejaculation—no fluid at all, let alone semen.

If you do not know the cause of this, in your drugged state you can suffer an anxiety, a terror not easy to describe. It feeds your despair the fact that you have become sexually injured somehow.

Do not tell one of the two prison psychiatrists who come by your cell door each morning. When his face looms into view at the window of your door, when he smiles like a mechanical man and says "How are you this morning?"—flee into yourself. Smile cheerfully and blink your eyes when you say "Fine, fine" —or he will *double* your dosage. They punish you if you bother them, if you report complications.

I can understand how a man's mind can be turned to steel in prison—only in this way can he be equal to the hardships that surround him.

Uncle Ho wrote this poem in prison:

> *Without the cold and desolation of winter*
> *There could not be the warmth and splendor of spring.*
> *Hardships have tempered and strengthened me,*
> *And turned my mind to steel.*

I have never forgotten this in about thirteen or fourteen years.

. . .When I became poetic about a prisoner's mind turning to *steel*, I meant to convey the idea of a *will power* "steeled" in trials and hardships so profound that the prisoner's mental resolution, his powers of "iron logic" have been enhanced and not weakened. An opposite effect of torture. I hardly meant the prisoner lost his own humanity.

I know how to live through anything they could possibly dish up for me. I've been subjected to strip-cells, blackout cells, been chained to the floor and wall; I've lived through the beatings, of course; *every* drug science has invented to "modify" my behavior—I have endured. Starvation was once natural to me; I have no qualms about eating insects in my cell or living in my body wastes if it means survival. They've even *armed* psychopaths and put them in punishment cells with me to kill me, but I can control that. When they say "what doesn't destroy me makes me stronger," that is what they mean. But it's a mistake to equate the results with being *strong*. I'm extremely flexible, but I'm not *strong*. I'm weakened, in fact. I'm tenuous, shy, introspective, and suspicious of everyone. A loud noise or a false movement registers like a four-alarm fire in me. *But I'm not afraid—and that is strange,* because I care very much about someday being set free and I want to cry when I think that I'll never be free. I want to cry for my brothers I've spent a lifetime with. Someday I will leave them and never return.

. . .And after it is all done to you, after you have been robbed completely of fear and nothing anyone can threaten you with can constrain you—what point is served by keeping you in prison?

It is no longer *possible* to punish you. You have been rendered unpunishable. Madness is the only possible point in keeping you in prison. Or old age.

But for some perverse reason—I do not know *why*—I have never been twisted into insanity. I have come close to it many times—have in fact entered insanity—but it turns out that it was only an introductory affair. I always bounce back to sanity.

I have reached such a pass by now, I can sense derangement a long way off—I can see its most subtle expressions even in men not considered insane.

If I were a pole of a magnet and insanity a like pole, this image would express the matter. I cannot be pulled by it, but I know it by repulsion: by the force that repels me before I am even conscious it is there.

THE HOLE:
SOLITARY CONFINEMENT

THERE IS only *one man* in a cell in the hole for it to really be "the hole." There are rows of cells on a tier, but in the hole —the genuine hole—no two prisoners are ever out of their cells at the same time.

There are always voices in the hole. It's a strange thing. I have seen *wars* take place in the hole. I have seen sexual love take place in the hole. I have seen, as a matter of fact, the most impossible things *happen* under these conditions. Let us say a kind of movement that is not really movement exists there. To illustrate: to walk ten miles in an enclosed space of ten feet is not really movement. There are not ten miles of space, only time. You do not go ten miles. To write about the hole, in other words, I would have to explore such common places.

. . .I have been dragged to the hole fighting back many times. I was once carried to the hole in Leavenworth by the security force (goon squad). My hands were cuffed behind me. A pig about six feet two inches who weighed about two hundred and fifty pounds was the boss. He was about forty-five, but he was hard as a rock. The pigs had me face down on the concrete floor, punching and kicking me. It was exactly like a pack of dogs on me. The big one, the boss, ordered me to stand up. He motioned to the others to stand back—and I swear to God, you won't believe this, he knocked my clothes off me with a few swipes of his hands.

The cloth tore my skin like knife cuts. I hit the floor, he hit my shoes (high tops) and knocked them off (broke the laces). All through this thing I tried to keep my head by acting passive and smiling. I thought they were so afraid of me it made them animals, which was true, but I couldn't calm them. That was the time they threw me face down in a dungeon cell. They stood on me while one unhandcuffed me. The pig who knocked my clothes off was the last to leave the cell. I heard them back out of the cell and I rolled over onto my side. I was hurting everywhere. Well, this pig, who had seemed the least emotional of them all, had his cock out and his face was wrinkled up in a grin and he kind of bounced up and down by bending his knees. He was pretending to jerk off. Then he zipped his fly and left the cell kind of chuckling.

. . .You sit in solitary confinement stewing in nothingness, not merely your own nothingness but the nothingness of society, others, the world. The lethargy of months that add up to years in a cell, alone, entwines itself about every "physical" activity of the living body and strangles it slowly to death, the horrible decay of truly living death. You no longer do push-ups or other physical exercises in your small cell; you no longer pace the four steps back and forth across your cell. You no longer masturbate; you can call forth no vision of eroticism in any form, and your genitals, like the limbs of your body, function only to keep your body alive.

Time descends in your cell like the lid of a coffin in which you lie and watch it as it slowly closes over you. When you neither move nor think in your cell, you are awash in pure nothingness.

Solitary confinement in prison can alter the ontological makeup of a stone.

. . .My years in solitary confinement altered me more than I care to admit, even to myself. But I will try to relate the experience, because you're understanding, and what you do not understand is only what you cannot because *you* have not experienced the hole for years. You *listen* and that is all that counts.

It is hard for me to begin. Beginnings are like that for me now.

But something happens down there in the hole, something like an event, but this event can only occur over a span of years. It cannot take place in time and space the way we ordinarily know them.

Not many prisoners have experienced this event. It *never* fails: most prisoners I know who have been in prison off and on all their lives will tell you they have served *five years* in the hole. Everyone is lying, and I do not know why they must say they served *five years* in the hole. Why *five years?* I cannot understand why that particular duration occurs to all of them. They do not say "I served *four years* or *three years*"—nor even six or seven years. It is *always* five years. I *do* know perhaps a half dozen who *have* indeed served five years or six years, but they are so few and so far between.

At any rate, let me return to the point. Let us say you are in a cell ten feet long and seven feet wide. That means seventy feet of *floor* space. But your bunk is just over three feet wide and six and a half feet long. Your iron toilet and sink combination covers a floor space of at least three feet by two feet. All tallied, you have approximately forty-seven square feet of space on the floor. It works out to a pathway seven feet long and about three feet wide—the excess is taken up by odd spaces between your commode and wall, between the foot of the bunk and the wall.

If I were an animal housed in a zoo in quarters of these dimensions, the Humane Society would have the zookeeper arrested for cruelty. It is illegal to house an animal in such confines.

But I am not an animal, so I do not insist on such rights.

My body communicates with the cell. We exchange temperatures and air currents, smells and leavings on the floor and walls. I try to keep it clean, to wash away my evidence, for the first year or two, then let it go at that.

I have experienced everything possible to experience in a cell in a short time—a day or so if I'm active, a week or two if I'm sluggish.

I must fight, from that point on, the routine, the monotony that will bury me alive if I am not careful. I must do that, and do it without losing my mind. So I read, read anything and everything. So I mutter to myself sometimes; sometimes recite poetry.

I have my memories. I have the good ones, the bad ones, the ones that are neither of these. So I have *myself*.

I have my seven-by-three-feet pathway, and I pace, at various speeds, depending on my mood. I think. I remember. I think. I remember.

Memory is arrested in the hole. I think about each remembered thing, study it in detail, over and over. I unite it with others, under headings for how I feel about it. Finally it changes and begins to tear itself free from facts and joins my imagination. Someone said *being is memory*.

It travels the terrain of time in a pure way, unfettered by what is, reckless of what was, what will become of it. Memory is not enriched by any further experience. It is *deprived* memory, memory deprived of every movement but the isolated body traveling thousands of miles in the confines of my prison cell.

My body plays with my mind; my mind plays with my body; the further I go into that terrain of time, into my memories, the more they enter my imagination. The imagination—bringing this memory into that, and that into this, every possible permutation and combination—replaces further experience, which would, if not enhance it, at least leave it intact.

I remember well, with such clarity, I am blinded by the memory. It is as if I had forgotten—but it is that I remember so well, too well:

Why am I here? Because I needed the money? Or was it the palmprint on the counter? What was it—a theft? Or was it that girl by the pond in the flowery dress who smiled at me . . .?

Where was I?

Every memory has an element of pain or disappointment. It scolds a little and in its own way. These elements are normally overshadowed by a familiarity we can live with— we happily forget the rest. The rest: there is no rest—but a quality we can live with in comfort, a degree of quietude.

In the hole after a while the painful elements begin to throw out shoots and sprout like brittle weeds in the garden of memory—until finally, after so long, they choke to death everything else in the garden.

You are left with a wild wasteland of scrubby weeds and flinty stone and dusty soil. They call it *psyche-pain*.

It is the same with ideals. Everyone has a few: a touch of idealism, a little of passion. As life in the hole, in the pure terrain of time, continues, your passions are aroused less and less with the help of memories and more and more by your ideals. Love, Hate, Equality, Justice, Freedom, War, Peace, Beauty, Truth—they all eventually become Idols, pure and empty abstract gods that demand your fealty, your undying obedience. Little Hitlers come from every precious feeling, every innocent notion you ever entertained, every thought about yourself, your people, the world—all become so many idols, oblivious to each other, that stridently dictate to you in the prison hole.

You cannot fill them up with your days, your years, for they are empty too. But you try—God, how you try.

The wasteland that is your memory now comes under the absolute dictatorship of idols too terrible to envision.

They are the hard, driving winds that torture the tumbleweeds across the prairie desert of memory—the crazy, hard winds that whip up smaller chaotic columns of dust that twist a few feet in the air like little tornadoes. They are the scorching suns that wither the scrubby vegetation and torture the air that shimmers in waves of suffocating heat that rises from the dead, hard stone. They are the cold, merciless nights of the desert that offer surcease only to the fanged serpents: the *punishment* unfolds.

Don't go near yourself.

Then the mirages in the wasteland. You are far from insanity; you are only living through an experience, an event. The mirages are real reflections of how far you have journeyed into that pure terrain of time. They *are* real. They bring the now out-of-place things back into the desert that was once the felicitous garden of your memory. *There a cherished woman passes into existence and you approach, draw close to her, and you touch her and she caresses you and then she vanishes in a shimmer to reveal the man masturbating that you have become and are caressing so tenderly. A beautiful flower is seen at a small distance and opens its radiant wings in a promise of spring among the dusty weeds. More suddenly than it appeared, it disappears to reveal a dark splotch on the wall in the fetid, musky cell. A brook bubbles over the dusty pebbles of the wasteland, promising to quench, to quench—and as you turn, it disappears in a flush of the toilet.*

Anything you can experience in the hole, you do to yourself, and after an indecent interval, each occasional experience recalls the old, nice quality of a memory which lies fallow be-

neath the wasteland. A word in a sentence; a tone in a voice
or sound; a fleeting essence in a taste or odor; a momentary
texture in a tactile sensation, or a combination of motion and
form and color caught by the tail of your visual field. These can
revive a good thing. Real things: these are the mirages in the
desert.

The real world is out of place in the hole, but the hole is
nonetheless really there. It is time that no longer moves forward in human experience. You can walk, placing one foot
before the other, across eternity in time. All the space you need
is six or seven feet. The hole furnishes only that provision: you
are living a demonstration of the theory of the infinite within
the finite; the dream within the reality.

But the hole is not the stuff of dreams, of fantasies: it is all
quite real. In fact, it is so real it haunts you.

Experience occurs seldom and only in extremes: vividly intense or drably monotonous. Surreal paintings have tried to
capture—with some success, I might add—the relationships
that are very real in life in the prison hole. It is *not* a dream.
To you it is not a dream. Your words and thoughts can only
reflect this condition of your sensations, your feelings; they do
not know their plight. Few thoughts in the hole are conscious
of their true grounds.

You become silent, contemplative, because you have become inverted. Your sense perception, having taken in everything, including yourself, within the finite confines of the hole,
passes through the monotony and now rises up from the *other*
side, the infinite, to haunt you with reality. Those outside the
hole, at that moment, would call it a dream—but you inside
the hole are in reality, not a dream:

What am I? Do I exist? Does the world exist? Will I
awaken to find this is all a dream? Is there a God? Am I the
devil? What is it like to be dead? What does toilet water
taste like? What is it like to put a finger up my butt? What
would happen should I shit on the floor? Or piss down my
legs? Am I homosexual? What is it like to sleep on this
filthy concrete floor?

The mind deprived of experience because of social sensory deprivation in the hole conceives its intellectual faculty to be capable of putting to use a fictional apparatus in the brain. It will believe that somehow it can learn to control this apparatus and use it to move material things, to destroy or change or create physically real things. Shorn of a gracious God, the mind surrenders to nothing, to Nothingness:

If I concentrated, could I melt or bend the bars of my cell? (Yes. Ommmm.) Should I first try to concentrate to move that scrap of dust on the floor? (Yes. Ommmm.) Did it move? (I saw it move just a hair.)

The intelligence recedes, no more a tool of learning—because knowledge is based on experience—but a tool of the outside world it is deprived of knowing. It tries to contact other minds by telepathy; it becomes the Ancestor. *Words* and *Numbers* come to hold mystic significance: they were invented by some arcane magic older than man. The line between the word and the thing vanishes; the intervals of numbers in infinity collapse with infinity.

The mind now crouches in fear and superstition before the idols of the hole, terrified:

I do not want to talk any more. There is nothing you can say of interest. I cannot remember ever being happy. No one has ever been kind to me. Everyone betrays me. No one can possibly understand—they are too ignorant. You have not suffered what I have endured. You call me names (homosexual). You do not understand. You mock me (screwball). This world is nothing. An illusion. Death is the release.

But a kind of genius can come of this deprivation of sensation, of experience. It has been mistaken as naïve intelligence, when in fact it is *empty* intelligence, pure intelligence. *The composition of the mind is altered.* Its previous cultivation is disintegrated and it has greater access to the *brain, the body:* it is Supersanity.

Learning is turned inside out. You have to start from the top and work your way down. You must study mathematical theory before simple arithmetic; theoretical physics before applied physics; anatomy, you might say, before you can walk.

You have to study philosophy in depth before you can understand the simplest categorical differences assumed in language or in any simple commonplace moral or ethical maxim.

Indeed, it is almost a rule that the more simple and commonplace something is, the more difficult to understand it.

You have come the full circle; experienced that single event that happens down there in the prison hole. How long does it take? Years. I would say five years or more.

. . .They finally put a name on what I have suffered in solitary: *sensory deprivation.* The first few times I served a couple of years like that, I saw only three or four drab colors. I felt only concrete and steel. When I was let out, I could not orient myself. The dull prison-blue shirts struck me, dazzled me with a beauty they never had. All colors dazzled me. A piece of wood fascinated me by its feel, its texture. The movements of things, the many prisoners walking about, and their multitude of voices—all going in different directions—bewildered me. I was slow and slack-jawed and confused—but beneath the surface I raged.

I can guess how wasted I have become now by the fact that I am no longer disoriented by solitary confinement. It has finally wormed its way into my heart: I cannot measure my deprivation any longer.

Let us say I can no longer measure my *feelings.* I can draw the proportions mentally, however.

. . .I explained to you the other day that the cell regulates the moods of the body. The mind does not regulate its own condition. Mental depression, for example, is a state of the mind caused by the body. In a cell in the hole it only *seems* that there is a separation of mind and body— in fact, the body's condition (of deprivations of sensations; experiences, functions, and so on) controls the moods of the mind more than in any other situation I can think of.

William James described this relationship when he said we become sad because we shed tears: we do not shed tears because we are sad. That is our original condition as living beings.

A long time ago in the hole, when I first entered prison, I was on the floor lying on my stomach writing a letter, with my elbows propping me up. So I was bent directly over the page I was writing on.

My mood was "normal"—I mean the normal mood of a prisoner in the hole. I remember I noticed, as I was writing, little spots of water appearing on the paper. I touched them with a finger and wondered at the phenomenon—when suddenly I realized tears were falling from my eyes, and immediately I began to weep uncontrollably. It was the first and only time I have wept since I was a child. I do not know *why* now, nor did I know the cause of it then. I must have been weeping over everything, all of it.

. . .A man is taken away from his experience of society, taken away from the experience of a living planet of living things, when he is sent to prison.

A man is taken away from other prisoners, from his experience of other people, when he is locked away in solitary confinement in the hole.

Every step of the way removes him from experience and narrows it down to only the experience of himself.

There is a *thing* called death and we have all seen it. It brings to an end a life, an individual living thing. When life ends, the living thing ceases to experience.

The *concept* of death is simple: it is when a living thing no longer entertains experience.

So when a man is taken farther and farther away from experience, he is being taken to his death.

THE PRISON STAFF

THE PIGS in the state and federal prisons—especially in the judicial system—treat me so violently, I cannot possibly imagine a time I could ever have anything but the deepest, aching, searing hatred for them. I can't begin to tell you what they do to me. If I were weaker by a hair, they would destroy me.

. . .You asked about the way violence is inculcated in prisoners.

I have never come into bodily contact with another human being in almost twenty years except in combat; in acts of struggle, of violence.

How is it possible to do otherwise? Contact sports are not allowed in any prison I have been in.

. . .Can you envision what it is to be a victim of terrorism in the hole? At any moment the cell door can be flung open and guards can enter and beat you to the floor, even as you sleep. At any hour of any day.

In the so-called closed psychiatric wards of the federal medical center for prisoners when I was there, it was done *routinely.* No prisoner had to say a word or do anything to bring on the terror.

The guards do not speak to you. You are *cattle,* without the faculty of reason. I have been pointed in the direction of a place across the floor or the exercise cage and given a push to get me to walk there because the guards, in their contempt, will not acknowledge that a prisoner can understand reason.

. . .The guards there at that time took it upon themselves to prescribe injections of phenothiazene drugs as potent as *Prolixin*—and every one of these drugs is *dangerous.* They will not *kill* you, but will most certainly cripple you. They in effect *lobotomize* you.

I was so constantly and arbitrarily attacked in my cell there, after a while my desire for physical relief was so powerful and all-pervading that when the guards finally would leave off the attack and exit my cell, I would sometimes achieve an erection out of despair and pain.

I have in those conditions had to masturbate to relieve myself, but not masturbate with any vision in my mind, my imagination. The pure physical act of caressing the penis after numberless exposures to attack is enough. It is entirely a physical thing, entirely involuntary.

Were I an ordinary man with ordinary misunderstandings, I could easily have misunderstood what was happening inside me. I could have misunderstood to the point of becoming a sexual masochist, or a sadist. I could very easily have confused this act of release with a sexual act of love, could have easily been twisted by this thing.

How many prisoners have been?

. . .Prisoners are inculcated by acts of violence so constant and detailed, so thorough and relentless, as to develop a kind of defensive automatic suspicion of everyone. This suspicion has been called *paranoic.*

It stems more from the indoctrinated belief prisoners come to have that every injury to them, they bring upon themselves.

They end up doing, almost consciously, suicidal violence to themselves, both mental and physical.

. . .*Free will:* this is the doctrine of the American judiciary when it insists prisoners are to blame for whatever harm is inflicted upon them by prisons.

This legal insistence indoctrinates even the finest minds in this country.

And yet a prisoner has no free will, or at least, let us say, has *less* free will than other men. No man ever chooses to injure himself, so long as he is in possession of his own faculties—especially if he is in possession of his "free will."

If I seize hold of a policeman who has, under the auspices of the judiciary, sent me to the prison hole because I do not like him and want him to leave me alone and I tell him so, is he to blame for an injury he sustains *from me?*

Ah, yes! He has no "free will"—he is an *impersonal tool of the government!* That is the way this twisted logic of American justice proceeds.

I have never seen an indifferent pig. I have seen lazy and unconcerned pigs, but *never* an objective and indifferent pig. The lazy ones are like magnanimous kings who carelessly overlook "slights" and arbitrarily pass out "mercies," but will, at a whim, suddenly rise up angry and take it all back, relegating everyone to hell.

Always, *always* every guard in prison is a tyrant, and prisoners are his subjects.

Is that the right of government founded by free men?

. . .In San Quentin—and many other prisons—if a guard on a gun-rail or in a gun-tower sees you *touch* another prisoner, he *will* shoot you down with his rifle. If he sees you *run* in the exercise yard, he *will* shoot you down. In the process, "stray" bullets *always* strike down other prisoners.

If the guards come to your cell to search it and before they can enter your cell you make a move toward your toilet, you *will* be shot down in your cell. They are "afraid" you will flush contraband down the toilet.

That is why San Quentin has the very best hospital for *traumatic medicine* in America. *Army* doctors even come there to learn.

Now, you just tell me who the fuck deserves to be subjected to all this as a *matter of justice*?!

. . .A prison warden or guard—*any* authority in a jail or prison—hates one thing worse than anything else, and that's a prisoner who is "arrogant." There is a way a convict can *walk, just walk by,* that's a challenge to a pig. A convict can give a pig a supreme insult just by standing and answering the pig without saying or doing anything you can put your finger on. There is a way of *looking* at them that they interpret as defiance. (They used to throw you in the hole for *looking* wrong; they called it "eyeballing.")

I haven't been on the main line (the yard) in any penitentiary in which I have caught the attention of a pig (especially a warden) and I haven't been stripped and searched *on the spot.*

The violence between guard and prisoner is open, naked, and you see a lot of prisoners defending themselves in fistfights with pigs.

I have never seen one pig whip one inmate. Not even two pigs can whip an average prisoner. When I speak of a prisoner fistfighting *pigs*—I mean that literally: at least five or six pigs at a time.

. . .The pigs tell the public they are at a disadvantage. How so? Well, you see: when they are in a fight with a convict, they say they can *only* apply "necessary force"; they cannot *beat him up*—because, you see, the law "forbids" it. Whereas a prisoner is not so restrained.

Not once in the judicial history of this country has the "law" forbade beating a prisoner in a fight—by "beating" I mean beating him *to death*. *Never.*

The law *does* forbid the methodical use of torture and corporeal punishment. How can anyone *prove* such practices exist when only *convicts* witness it?

No one in this country can cite for me a *single* instance in which a prisoner's complaint of cruel and unusual punishment *has ever* at any time been affirmed as true either by the government in general or the prison regime in particular. *Never* has it happened.

So tell me this: Why does no one *believe* the word of a prisoner over the word of the prison authorities?

I would like to know, because in every single instance in which a prisoner is lucky enough to air his complaint in a courtroom—in one of those civil rights lawsuits—he *always* has been vindicated. *Always* proven to have told the truth.

Never, not a single time, has a prisoner been shown in court to have been *lying* in his complaints of cruel and unusual punishment.

I think that this country has an excessive number of people who take *pride*—openly or secretly—in the fact that their government is so inhumane, so evil; take pride in the fact that their government so thoroughly crushes men they consider "enemies" ("public enemies").

And those who do not have this kind of pride in their government, only *sneer* at those who do. And do nothing more.

. . .An ex-cop was committed to prison. He had arrested someone I once knew. He was one of those typical belligerent pigs. I guess he was about thirty-five. Someone pulled up on him on the yard and told him what he knew of him. The cop begged him to keep it quiet. The man agreed. He set him up to get into debt with some prisoners I knew. When the cop ran out of money to pay them, he bought the debt. That meant he had *purchased the cop*. The cop was standing there big-eyed and scared shitless when it happened. Later the one who bought him and several of his partners were standing talking to me in the corridor. The cop was walking by. The one he owed called him over to us. He just looked at him and said, "I just sold your debt. You owe me nothing. You owe him." He indicated this man, who walked him all over the joint, making him get things on credit from a dozen different prisoners. The cop killed himself a few days later. For some reason he wouldn't ask for lock-up protection. That's what they wanted him to do. They didn't want to kill him.

This pig was so typical a dirty pig, he could have passed for the Georgian highway patrolman in the car commercial. Outside he used brutality to force information from people. I think he got his dues. It is unusual to see an ex-cop in a real penitentiary. Why this one made it there, I still am baffled. Someone high must have been very angry at him!

I doubt if there is today a *single* agency in the federal government that does not have its own little police force. Of course, this could be *my* "problem of perception." But I know the policeman *mentality* much, much better than that mentality is capable of knowing *mine*.

They use the old filing-system trick. They collect and *intentionally* manufacture so much bullshit about the citizenry—so much "top-secret" and "confidential" *shit*—they actually alarm those Bible-thumping, plastic-man politicians who get into office leading brass bands and kissing ass that they *shrink* before the rows of files and stacks of dossiers of *people* and *things*, which, if they were true, half of the American population would be under indictment—and if even a fraction of it was *false, they* would be indicted. So it is suppressed from public view.

Policemen do not have to "worry" about elections. That is not how they get into office. They *hire* one another. They make absolutely certain the job is so "complicated"—with their checks and counterchecks, their codes and signals, etc.—no one can do it but them. They do all the "investigating" of *each other:* all the phony cover-ups, gagging—murders.

. . .You said one of the weaknesses of my play is that I don't give anyone but prisoners *character.* You are absolutely correct. If it is a "weakness," it is the weakness of a *prisoner* writing about prison.

The guards *do not* have anything but "cold" characters. When they step out of being "cold characters," they inevitably become *obscenities.* And I could *never* portray them otherwise. Not in *truth.* I mean everyday empirical fact. *Yours* as well as mine.

That was the flaw in Cheever's book on prison. It is what tells me at bottom Cheever is extremely vain. To be so *sure* of the nature of the essential relationship between guards and their prisoners is pure foolishness. That is one of the things I like in you. You never extended such tempting presumptions.

The real relations are disturbing to the calm social mind. People like Cheever like to tell themselves guards and prisoners have points of congeniality. The truly horrifying thing is that they do not.

. . .Among themselves, the guards are human. Among themselves, the prisoners are human. Yet between these two the relationship is not human. *It is animal.* Only in reflection—subjective reflection—do they acknowledge sharing a common consciousness. What is that common consciousness? It is the consciousness that we belong to a *common species* of life. But this is not the consciousness of society. It is not humanistic; *it is animalistic.*

What I am saying is that the prisoner is closer to humanity than the guard: because he is *deprived* by the guard. That is why I say that evil exists—not in the prisoner, but in the guard. Intentions play none but an illusory role. *In fact,* the guard is evil. His *society* is demonic. I don't care if he likes the same food I do or the same music—or whatever: this is the illusory role intentions play. Animals can enjoy the same music or food we do.

Our actions define us.

Among themselves, these pigs are evil to the point of boredom. I've seen them among themselves; I've heard their talk. They are *extremely* venal. Extremely devoid of any trace of spirituality. Their dullness approaches the mentally defective. It is *fascist* The very symbol of injustice. It would seem to be an irony, but it is not: *prisoners do not make guards to be what they are.* Neither does society in general. The *state* does. It gives them *arbitrary* power over prisoners. They embrace it *as a way of life.* That is the source of their evil.

. . .It is much more difficult—and therefore it has a moralizing quality—for a prisoner to hurt or kill a guard than for a guard to hurt or kill a prisoner. The consequences to a prisoner are severe to a hellish degree. A guard gets a *medal* for it!

It has been my experience that injustice is perhaps the *only* (if not merely the *greatest*) cause of insanity behind bars. You'd be surprised to learn what a little old-fashioned oppression can do to anyone.

Here is how the average man views it:

He finds exceptions, and instead of acknowledging that these exceptions prove the rule, he substitutes the extremes, one for the other, and tells himself the *exception is evil* and not the rule: that guards are like anyone else at bottom, in spite of the brutal, evil *few.*

It is not true. Formal, temporal war (i.e., the phenomenon) reflects a deeper historical truth. And that truth is that there *is* such a thing as a relentless enemy in human society that requires eradication and cannot ever be reconciled with human society: the policeman mentality.

All human societies in history throughout the world have recognized this in the primitive (religious) consciousness of man's inhumanity to man.

Do you "sense" a common humanity in someone like Hitler? Or Himmler? If so, you are deluding yourself. They are not "family men" behind the scenes. They are not "ordinary people" in *any* aspect of their existence with others. Theirs was a revolution of policemen. *A revolution of the government.*

That is a hard truth to bear.

When Marx says the capitalist *is* the living incarnation of capital, this is what he understands. We are what we do and our thoughts reflect our actions. The idealists—like Hegel—hold the opposite view: the official human is a citizen of the State. The ultimate citizen is the Policeman.

I am not saying this state of affairs has always been with human society and that it will always be with human society. *Evil* emerged with the beginning of History and has now fully emerged into view. You can look at it, touch it—speak to it. It belongs to us to wipe it out. All religions reflect that struggle with evil.

All this content lies beneath the conscious intent of a communist revolutionary. It is not foremost in his mind because his task is not perceived as religious—but economic, political. He has not the luxury, the time, to delve into the religious meaning *now*.

But I, in prison so long, have found the time. This is why the communist movement has been haphazardly compared with a religious movement.

. . .If I wrote of a guard's "home life," it would be a study in domination of women and children. Their women and children do not *love* them; they worship them.

The only time they appear human is when you have a knife at their throats. The instant you remove it, they fall back into animality. Obscenity.

You think I just see "one side" of them? They have a "good side"—but as I said, *only* when there is a knife at their throats: *They obey violence.* They obey it in their hearts, as do all animals.

A prisoner does not.

A prisoner rebels even with the knife at his throat. That is why at this time he is a prisoner. It is the essence of being a prisoner today. He cannot be subdued. Only murdered.

This is true in spite of himself.

Those who are neither guards nor prisoners are nevertheless either oppressed or oppressors. There is not a true "mixture" of these two terms. There is always a principled contradiction.

There is a "gray area" inhabited by most people in European industrial societies. It is like the dry foliage that surrounds a fire that will spread and consume it. Everything in the world is committed to the flame, no matter our wishes.

When they come in their jackboots and kick in your door, that "gray area" of your existence will be no more. You will join in our struggles in spite of yourself.

The "gray area" deludes itself. Tells itself the conflict can resolve itself peacefully, or that it is not *real.*

You may call it "laziness"—others have called it "business as usual" and "apathy." If you were caught in the eye of a whirlwind, perhaps you could look out for miles across a peaceful countryside. You would know the whirlwind *would* tear the whole countryside apart. Know for certain. Know that *it will.* Someone in the countryside may be oblivious to it.

That is how I know a great conflagration is coming that will tear the whole world apart. And it is time to fight our enemies and not fool ourselves that they are not "really" enemies. It is time to join the conflagration to make certain our enemies do not prevail.

The industrial countries will enter it with the emergency of an off-on switch. But all the other countries in the world are *already* in it. They are burning and the fire is growing. It will consume the world.

There is no point in pretending our lifetimes will not in the end culminate in a world revolution.

That is the way I see it. That is how I look at tomorrow.

I wish it were otherwise, but nothing would convince me it isn't.

. . .There are wardens and prison guards in my life for whom the very notion that I should forgive them is insane. Retribution is a great part of the subjective condition for revolution. Call it vengence if you want.

A warden, a President Nixon, a Führer Hitler will never be one of us. History demands this, not just the human heart. We could never live side by side with such monsters—the day after the revolution—on equal terms. That is asking for too much. They must pay. Because we are not machines.

Because we are not machines, we cannot wait long enough for the so-called "economic development of the objective conditions" or "withering away" of the bourgeoisie.

There will be a "day after the revolution."

THE INMATES

WALKING INTO the new Maximum Security units is exactly like walking into a room lined with animal cages. Any prisoner has a full view of any other prisoner in his cell.

All day there are arguments and threats hollered all over the place. It is not too different, really, than the "monkey houses" or the zoo.

If one of the prisoners wants to, he can taunt you with insults and threats at any time, and you have no chance of silencing him. So you have to be careful not to get one of these punks running his mouth at you (for weeks on end sometimes). So you have to be friendly and "converse" with him about any fucked-up subject he wants. It is who can shout the loudest over the longest period who dominates this situation. It is the only situation I have knowledge of in which a scurrying coward can impose himself *directly* upon other men.

The *vileness* of such men is in no other case so exposed to view. There are not that many such men, but they dominate relations between men in cages.

All day, from breakfast to suppertime about four or five o'clock, the time is broken up by guards, and each death-row prisoner's door is opened onto the tier one at a time. At that time you can shower, sweep out your cell and pace the tier in front of the cells of others. Jonathan is demanding as a child. He will reach into your cell and shake you awake to talk excitedly about the Lone Ranger show, or some such. Nothing you can say to him will get him off your back. Next Thomas comes out. He hangs around your cell, smiling "meaningfully" and watching alternately your lower body and your eyes. He'll bring you his cigarettes and candy just to open a conversation. He'll ask you real nice to put your cock out through the bars to him. He won't be put off. He'll hound you, and there is nothing you can do but try to ignore him. You can't grab him and rattle his teeth; you can't reach anyone. Stephen isn't like that; he is introverted. Joseph paces and bumps into everything. You try to read, and find you've been reading the same paragraph for hours. The noise level is high. You can't think or concentrate.

The closest you come to adjusting is this: you *will* yourself to sleep all day through most of the disturbances. After each meal you curl up, pull the blankets over you, put your pillow over your ears and sleep. It's a drugged sleep. Once for about three years I slept like that sixteen hours a day.

When the lights go out you lie there, and relief comes only between midnight and breakfast. You stay up all night enjoying the tremendous relief. The noise which literally vibrates your brain is gone. The distractions disappear. The freaks' faces are not in front of your cell. You are with yourself again. Until dawn, at least.

But you can't read, you can't write. You can't listen to a radio. All you hear is the pigs making their rounds. You hear keys, chains, the dogs they bring in on the count. You hear the sleeping sounds of the prisoners. Every night there is at least one screaming out in his sleep. You pass the night thinking, remembering your life. You go back to your earliest memories, your first childhood memory, and advance to today. You've masturbated yourself to the point of total sexual uninterest months (years?) ago. You fantasize a lot. You think of your future, a future *you know* can never exist.

That's no way to *exist*, let alone *live*. You're exhausted from thinking, when dawn and breakfast come. You eat and fall asleep. The gate to your cell bangs open before you know it. You *stagger* out of bed, go through the motions of showering. You fall into bed again. No sooner are you asleep than lunch is served. You pick at it, half asleep. You finally tell the others in no uncertain terms to stay away from your cell front and not to speak to you. You threaten to throw a cup of urine on them, knowing you are taking a chance they'll do the same to you. If you're lucky, they'll keep their intrusions on you to a minimum. But you can't stop them completely. The tension wraps itself around your brain like a steel vise.

To live in "peace" in such circumstances can change you into one of those damned men who will do anything to live, to exist biologically.

It is only a matter of time, if you love life too much or fear violence too much, before you become a thing, no longer a man. You can end up scurrying about like a rodent, lending yourself to every conceivable low, evil, degrading act anyone tells you to do—either pigs or prisoners.

There is a boundary in each man. He can eat crow and brown-nose to an extent. He can shuck the man for a while, become a good "actor."

But when a man goes beyond the last essential boundary, it alters his ontology, so to speak. It's like the small pebble that starts a landslide no one can stop. You can betray the pigs until, lo, you've betrayed yourself. You want to survive so badly, to be free of violence so terribly, you will literally do anything after you start across that boundary. You'll allow *anyone* to order you around. You'd let your ma, wife, kids die just to stay alive yourself. You'll wallow in the gutter of man's soul to live.

You'll suck every cock in the cell house to "get along." There is nothing you won't do.

Most convicts don't cross that line. Those who do never return again. You accept violence, committing it to survive *morally* as well as biologically. You're not a "psycho," a killer. That doesn't mean you won't kill, you won't do mind-boggling acts of violence. It is hard to bring yourself to these acts, but you take a deep breath, look intelligently at what you must do, and you do it even though you are scared stiff and sick to your stomach.

. . .Myself and my fellow prisoners lived a hard code, but it was one of survival. Survival of dignity and sanity. If we didn't, we would truly be broken completely.

The only thing a convict respects in another is moral strength. That is all it takes to kill a man. I don't fear or respect any man only for his ability to harm another, and no convict does.

But in prison there are many broken men. I've seen them wince when a pig walks by. I've seen them break down to stuttering so bad they can't talk. I've seen them go from day to day existing entirely with only the need, fulfilled daily, of constant oral copulation. These are the ones so demeaned and broken by the violence of things, there is nothing they won't do short of any act involving violence. If they were unafraid of violence, they would not have lost their humanity.

. . .The "working code" of a convict is at bottom to best the man, the pig. To do what he can to get his time done and get out of prison. There are some things he can't do and still be a man (a convict). At that point, he rebels. He has no "revolutionary ideology," true. But eventually he'll run into me in the hole and I'll tell him things that will clear this confusion and give his rebellion a cause. It's happening all over the country now. It's a new breed of convict. And when he rebels alone, if I see him fighting a squad of pigs on the yard or in the hole, I will never hesitate to dive in. We are brothers under the skin. His fight is my fight. If I pay the highest price for helping him and he later cops out, it doesn't bother *me*. I've done right and I have no bad feelings for him. We got no one but each other, and I learned that a long time ago.

. . .The murder of a pig in prison is worse by far than the assassination of the President of the U.S.A. At least then you have the hope of walking the prison yard. No one kills a guard and ever walks a prison yard again. He is never released from the hole.

I had a friend we called Striker. He murdered a guard in front of everyone. Murdered him right in the main run in the big cell house.

A lot of things conspired to bring him to that. First of all, he had been in prison for twenty-three solid years. But he was only forty years of age. The day previous his mother had died; had, as they say, "expired" quietly in her sleep of old age. It was all he had left outside prison.

He was a poor poker player. He was playing poker in the main run in the cell house with several others. A new pig walked past and stopped and ordered them to break up the game. Poker is against the rules, but the pigs let it go on as long as they see that all the poker players are "regulars," i.e., as long as no "weak" inmates are sitting at the table. The new guard did not know this.

Striker had been drinking pruno, and when he does this he *always* without fail becomes belligerent. He argued with the pig, but the pig insisted and threatened to throw him in the hole. Striker tried to recruit the other players to keep on playing to defy the pig, but since he was the only loser, they quit playing.

Someone told Striker that since he was so angry, why not just kill the pig? He was half-joking when he told Striker this, but

Striker grabbed at it and vowed that he would kill the pig except that he had no knife.

The prisoner, more to get rid of Striker, to get him out of his hair more than anything, gave him a knife. It was overall about fourteen inches in length, double-edged and a lethal-looking thing.

The pig was standing in the run with another pig in the midst of teeming inmates going to and fro. Striker pulled up beside the pig and hung about ten inches of that knife into his belly and gutted him. The other pig spun around to face Striker and was hit in the stomach several times as he ran backward to get away. Then Striker turned back to the other pig and stabbed him again with long deep thrusts in the chest area.

The pig was now flat on his back, bleeding like a fountain. Everyone stood in arrested movements, watching. Striker knew what he had done and he looked about him wildly for help, and then he was seen to smile. He went to his knees and began speaking to the dying pig.

He sunk the knife into the middle of his chest and said, "How do you like that?" as he twisted the knife from side to side. Then he pulled it out and began sawing off the pig's head.

By then there were about fifty guards on the scene, and so Striker did as he was told and dropped the knife and walked off, with them escorting him to the hole. They were *all* in a worse state of shock than Striker even.

Striker received a life sentence and was transferred to the hole at another Maximum Security penitentiary.

Shortly thereafter, in the middle of the night, he was found hanged in his cell. There are stories that the guards lynched him, but Striker told me he would have to kill himself, and if he could have cried, he would have when he told me that. Because I agreed with him. Mercy is sometimes the hardest thing in the world because real mercy requires an act of personal atonement. He was thoughtless enough to have done it: killed a pig in such a way that he had to be caught at it.

There was another act of mercy I was party to once. There was a convict, about fifty-five years old, named X. He had a series of heart attacks, and the last stroke left him totally paralyzed except for one eyelid. He was serving a life sentence.

I was with someone when he went to the infirmary to visit his friend X. At that time he asked X to flick his eyelid once for yes and twice for no. They communicated like that for a while. I did not pay much attention to what transpired.

Then he asked X if he wanted him, as his friend, to kill him, to put him out of the misery of not being able to care for himself in prison. I riveted my attention on them.

I looked at X's face. It was frozen like stone, like a death mask. For a long time we stood watching X's eyes. Finally I pulled my attention from X and glanced away momentarily, and then I looked back.

His eye was closed. Then it flicked back open again, and I watched carefully, in great suspense, for the other flick of the eyelid which would mean *no*. I did not know if that was the *second* flick of his eyelid, or the first. In any case, it was the last.

He just stared, as always, at the ceiling, as if it were a big screen that held the projection of scenes from Hell. He never did wink his eye again, and we left. I said nothing to this man. He usually talks a lot, but after that he only spoke when he had something to say because X somehow got turned over in his bed and smothered to death with his face in his pillow. That was the gist of his death report.

His friend killed him out of mercy in spite of the risk it took. I even asked him once if he killed X, and he looked at me hard in the eyes, looked at me with icy eyes, and in a cold voice said "Yes." And that was it. He walked away.

Is the fate of the man who handed Striker the knife and the man who killed X tied somehow to that of Striker's and X's?

Since then, I recall seeing those two men at a distance now and then. There is something in their bearing that indicates a conscious effort not to ever vacillate, not to ever have doubts about what they do. It is not easy for a man to kill his brother.

Some people say this is being "unreasonable," but they fail to understand that the past is never dead, never over and done with. What happens in the past is the future, and so the past is not static, fixed. Human reality is like that. The events and decisions in a personal history slide in and out of perspective, take on new meanings, just as the person does. For this very reason, there is no absolute *personal* good or evil.

They sometimes pause and stand next to me, and always they are looking everywhere but at me when they say "What's happening, Jack?" in greeting. Maybe once every year or so.

Only after saying this do they turn their face to me and level their eyes at mine. Eye to eye, I am studied carefully. Then they soften and put the look of a friend in their eyes and say, with genuine concern: "Is everything all right?"

Sometimes I just nod or I say "Yeah." Then they look away and they walk off again. It is as if they were just checking to see if, or how much, the past has changed since they were there last. I try not to change too much.

. . .There is no "camaraderie" among prisoners as a whole any more; there is a system, a network of ties between all the tips (prison cliques) in the prisons, and it's this that resembles "comradeship" in general. Most prisoners fear almost *every* other prisoner around them.

. . .As long as I've been in the *penitentiary* (jails are different) all the fistfights I've seen can almost be counted on one hand. You *never* see violence in the open and it's always with a knife or a piece of pipe (lately, here they use gasoline—dousing the enemy and igniting him). This, of course, refers only to the violence of prisoner against prisoner.

. . .It is, as a spectacle, a form of art which partakes of the elements of the auto-da-fé and the drama. Barbarian civilization invented it first as a way to make of punishment a spectator's sport and it developed its fullest expression in the gladiator games. Then the emergence of the civil nation-states broke it down and could have no room in society for such *barbarities*. So, you see, the bullfight is by no means a sport. The matador does not even see it this way, unless he is confused as to what he is doing. A bullfighter pursues it as an art form, almost the way a professional actor pursues drama.

In a bullfight a man risks his life to kill, but there is more: if he does not acquit himself with honor, he *loses;* the bull will prevail and he will be killed or maimed. The situation in the bullring demands great control. The bullfighter must *torment* the bull to bring out its fighting qualities and heighten them. The situation is such that it is *easier* for a bullfighter to kill a *brave* bull than a *cowardly* bull. If the bull is cowardly, then it is not a *bullfight*—it is a slaughter, and the matador dishonors himself when he stoops to the role of a *butcher*.

It is not a *sport* because it brings into play esthetic, sublime qualities which move men to contemplate *moral* elements of the spectacle, the way drama does in theatre.

The bullfighter retains, from the historical origins of bullfighting, a *gladiatorial* aspect—but what normal man would pursue such a thing!? The answer is this: men from near-penniless social classes; powerless men; men for whom bullfighting is a path to social attainments otherwise unattainable.

The qualities that are brought out in the bull—bravery, respect (at bottom, *honor*), intelligence (animal cunning heightened in combat with an intelligent adversary), and more —these qualities are emulated by the human male. So the matador is in a sense fighting another man to the death. It is a surrogate gladiator conflict.

A great matador is like an ingenious maestro who can bring out excellence in the most inexperienced of musicians by sheer dint of the talent he sees in them.

When the matador brings the bull to its highest grandeur, the animal becomes ideally *ennobled,* and in a moment of truth—because ideally at that juncture the matador and the bull become *equal*—the matador pierces its heart.

It is no accident that convicts speak of penal institutions for young men as *gladiator schools*. In such places, circumstances teach men *how* to kill one another. They are taught the way the *bull* is taught—through *torment*.

When a bull is brought to the bullring, he is brought directly from the fields of a ranch. He has no prior experience of the cape, of the play of a matador, nor even of a corral. It is a totally alien experience.

Every phase of a bullfight is a test. Before the bull confronts the matador, he is met with *peons*, and he whirls on them and sharp spears *(pics)* are imbedded in his neck muscles. He does not flee and hide; he ignores the pain, if he is brave, and attacks. Then men on horseback surround him and torment him, and he charges at them, again and again. His rage is blind.

If he is a good bull, he has passed all the tests. The *banderilleros*, the men on horseback, withdraw and the matador beckons from the center of the ring.

With his manner and his cape he draws the bull out into the center of the ring, and the bull is manipulated until his rage has reached such a peak that it is transformed into glory—enlightened by the figure of the matador.

The farther he is driven, the more self-contained he becomes; his confusion is transformed by the combat into a kind of intelligence crowned with valor.

What an experience for the bull! It must be of greater intensity than a religious experience. After this, he could never return to the herd from which he was taken. He could never again live as he did before. He would carry within him, all his days, the arena, the bullring.

If he wins—and the chances are almost nil that he will win —he will face bullfighters until one kills him.

Convicts who have been trained in *gladiator schools* acquit themselves with the honor of the tormented—with the honor with which the bull behaves in the bullring.

The only real difference is that the bull sinks into the dust of the bullring in a sea of voices chanting 'Bravo! Ole!'—amid a fragrant shower of roses that float down to him from the stands.

The prisoner dies in shame amid contemptuous and scorning men.

Sometimes a prisoner who happens to be physically big is encouraged to run the other prisoners' lives. That is the traditional dream of the typical warden. A hierarchy he can control. The big prisoners who believe this are usually fools who have been led (like sheep to the slaughter) to believe that because they can overpower with their hands the average man, everyone will obey them. What throws a wrench into all of this is the little skinny kid with a knife or some other weapon. The restraints, inner and outer, that govern ordinary men do not affect a prisoner bent on protecting himself.

To a prisoner it is an insult to grapple hand-to-hand with anyone. If someone ever strikes him with his hand (another prisoner), he has to kill him with a knife. If he doesn't, he will be fistfighting with him every day. He might be killed.

In prison we are all polite to each other: formal in our respect. We are serving years. If I have a verbal disagreement with someone, and I'm in the wrong, my apologies are given sincerely. But if I'm in the right and some asshole is wrong and he knows it, I have to see his face every day. If he threatened to kill me, I have to see him day in, day out for years. This is what leads to killing him over a seemingly trivial matter. *All the violence in prison is geared for murder,* nothing else. You can't have someone with ill feelings for you walking around. He could drop a knife in you any day.

You learn to "smile" him into position. To *disarm* him with friendliness. So when you are raging inside at anyone, you learn to conceal it, to smile or feign cowardice.

You have to move into total activity from a totally inactive posture to sink a knife in as close to his heart as possible. It is this that also unsettles a man's mind in prison. A knife is an intimate weapon. Very personal. It unsettles the mind because you are not killing in physical self-defense. You're killing someone in order to live respectably in prison. Moral self-defense.

Let's say someone steals something from your cell. You

catch him cold. Maybe he stole a carton of cigarettes. He gets loud with you. What you must do next is to become friendly with him. If he took your property, there is no telling what he may try to take next. It's possible that he would even try to fuck you if you let him steal from you. In prison society you are expected to put a knife in him. You might have to walk the yard with him for a week to take him off guard, to get him alone to kill him.

Here is how it is: You are both alone in his cell. You've slipped out a knife (eight- to ten-inch blade, double-edged). You're holding it beside your leg so he can't see it. The enemy is smiling and chattering away about something. You see his eyes: green-blue, liquid. He thinks you're his fool; he trusts you. You see the spot. It's a target between the second and third button on his shirt. As you calmly talk and smile, you move your left foot to the side to step across his right-side body length. A light pivot toward him with your right shoulder and the world turns upside down: you have sunk the knife to its hilt into the middle of his chest. Slowly he begins to struggle for his life. As he sinks, you have to kill him fast or get caught. He will say "Why?" Or "No!" Nothing else. You can feel his life trembling through the knife in your hand. It almost overcomes you, the gentleness of the feeling at the center of a coarse act of murder. You've pumped the knife in several times without even being aware of it. You go to the floor with him to finish him. It is like cutting hot butter, no resistance at all. They always whisper one thing at the end: "Please." You get the odd impression he is not imploring you not to harm him, but to do it right. If he says your name, it softens your resolve. You go into a mechanical stupor of sorts. Things register in slow motion because all of your senses are drawn to a new height. You leave him in the blood, staring with dead eyes. You strip in your cell and destroy your clothing, flushing it down the toilet. You throw the knife away. You jump under the showers. Your clarity returns. There is no doubt you did the only thing you could. Most of the regulars know you did it. No one questions, but whenever you see one, he may embrace you, pat your back, laugh. You just downed a rat everyone hates. In the big prisons, such murders are not even investigated at all. In _____, when I was there, between thirty and forty bodies were found stabbed to death. There was only one conviction, and even then, it was because the killer turned himself in and pleaded guilty to ten years.

I'm not a professional writer, so it is hard to write these things without sounding like a callous punk with a faulty imagination. But you want to stop in the middle of it and hold him so tight you can force his life back into him and save him. But you can't turn around in the middle of it. It's the unreason of violence, this time in favor of life, that tries to stop you in the act—the same force which brought you to this act.

. . .I tell you I was *there!* But I have seen it enough times to know it is *common.* He could have protected himself. Not only that, I have seen him *move* and I know he could have successfully defended himself. The one stabbing him was a *coward.*

He had only been slashed—not deeply—across the belly and his right shoulder. But his assailant shouted a command: "Drop your arms!"—and he looked at him bewildered *and dropped his arms to his sides.* He *offered* him his chest; actually filled his lungs, almost like a sigh of relief, pushing his chest out. Totally undefended. The man wasted no time taking his heart. He let the man *kill* him. He did not even try to *flee* for his life: He *gave* it to him. He all but said: "Here is my life, take it!"

. . .I have seen men stand as though frozen and I have seen them strain and try to fight their way out of their *own* passivity, all the while they are being cut down. All this just to be able to confront and overcome the violence which is already taking their lives.

When they finally do (if they do) begin to fight back, it is always too late. They are mortally wounded. They begin to flail about them, to try to appraise their attacker—but it is too late.

I'm not speaking of the shock of surprise. I'm not speaking of a moment's hesitation. I am saying they *accept* too easily their death at the hands of another. God, it sometimes even

becomes a *conscious acceptance,* at some point in their struggle
with themselves to overcome their own passivity.

. . .You *can* become so consumed with impotent hatred, so
enraged at someone or something in prison, you must *masturbate* to the violence taking place in your mind, because if you
cannot contain it *somehow,* if you loosen the grip on yourself
a little, you may start by speaking out, loudly—and end your
days in a screaming, raging froth from which there is no return.
You will leave this world *berserk.*

. . . .You relate the notion that violence is associated with
sexuality. It is an absurdity, but I agree to an extent.
. . .It is an absurd contradiction in (at least) American society
for a man to see the sexual penetration of his wife (or female
companion) as a consecration and expression of love—and
then to see this *same* act of penetration, but of another male,
as just the opposite: a *desecration* and expression of the deepest
contempt. It is because of this contradiction that sexuality is
so profoundly wed to violence.
One of the first things that takes place in a prison riot is this:
guards are sexually dominated, usually sodomized. I'm not pretending I do not "understand" this; we all do. I disagree on
several points that this is "natural" and that all overt acts of
sexual aggression fit the concept of *violence,* because violence
is *destructive.* There are those who entertain such acts out of
love. But what is clear is that when a man sodomizes another
to express his *contempt,* it demonstrates only his contempt for
woman, not man. The normal attitude among men in society
is that it is a great shame and dishonor to have experienced
what it feels like to be a woman. I think such a radical attitude
reflects *strong* feelings in the matter.

. . .I was sent to prison for the same reason Caryl Chessman
was executed: arrogance.

The judge sentenced me to the main penitentiary for the express purpose of having me raped by prisoners and reduced to a homosexual—this "version" being a *punk*. There was absolutely no other reason. At that time, there was not even a pretense of rehabilitation or a caseworker staff in prison. The prison was entirely presided over by old-school prison guards. There were no "rehabilitation" programs.

I was even told by the pigs who transported me to the prison that I was being sent there to be reduced to a punk, to be shorn of my manhood. They had felt I would be less arrogant once I had been turned into a cocksucker.

If I was afraid, I was never aware of it. It is certain that I was consumed with rage, the anger of deep insult. I arrived in that emotional and mental condition. You could say I was *paranoid:* bloodthirsty to establish my place.

New prisoners were placed in quarantine for about six weeks. Quarantine was called *fish-tier.* Someone I knew from the reform school slipped me a boning knife when I arrived on *fish-tier.*

The first prisoner—a middle-aged convict—who tried to fuck me, I drew my knife on. I forced him to his knees, and with my knife at his throat, made him perform fellatio on my flaccid penis in front of three of his partners.

This is the way it is done. If you are a man, you must either kill or turn the tables on anyone who propositions you with threats of force. It is the *custom* among young prisoners. In so doing, it becomes known to all that you are a man, regardless of your youth.

I had been trained from a youth spent in *gladiator school* for this. It was inevitable then that a youth in an adult penitentiary at some point will have to attack and *kill*, or else he most certainly will become a punk—even though it may not be well known he is a punk. If he cannot protect himself, someone else will.

Before I was twenty-one years old I had killed one of the prisoners and wounded another. I never did get out of prison. I was never a punk.

To the authorities, there is nothing seriously wrong with

anyone getting raped in prison. On the contrary, the idea excites them; they *enjoy* it.

In prison, if I take a punk, *she is mine.* He is like a slave, a chattel slave. It is the custom that no one addresses her directly. He cleans my cell, my clothing and runs errands for me. Anything I tell him to do, he must do—exactly the way a wife is perceived in some marriages even today. But I can sell her or lend her out or give her away at any time. Another prisoner can take her from me if he can dominate me.

. . .The majority of prisoners I have known—something like ninety percent—express sexual interest in their own sex. I hesitate to call this "homosexual" because American society recognizes *only* the passive homosexual—the one who plays the female role—as being a "homosexual." So it is really the same outside as in prison, but open in prison.

So you can see already how this distorts a lot of meanings and can fuel a lot of violence, both physical and psychological. Because no prisoner really respects a homosexual, and yet—as I said—almost all have these desires themselves. It is the same as in the society of men outside prison.

Also, in all the penitentiaries I have been transferred to, in each one there were only at most half a dozen "known" homosexuals among prisoners.

Only once or twice in my life have I seen in any prison two men demonstrate sexual affection by kissing or otherwise touching each other. The open homosexual plays the role of a woman and is usually the wife of a prisoner respected on the yard. He gives her the security and protection he would a woman outside prison. But to be a punk is surpassed in contempt only by being a snitch. Prison regimes respect these relationships. In reality they encourage them.

When a bull is selected from the herds that occupy the fields of a ranch for the bullring, care must be taken to observe how he relates to other bulls in the herd. A bull who displays confusion around other bulls at homosexual tendencies in himself is already defeated by males, by other bulls. He is *passive*, in spite of exhibiting the greatest outward masculine appearance. He is not just unsure of himself, his heart is subjugated by the male.

In men, this is the *prime* reason that in regular positional warfare—particularly, classical European warfare—the soldier discovered to be homosexual is executed. Homosexuals are exempt from conscription—at least from the battlefield.

Gerard fell to his knees before the bars of my cell and he pleaded with me, pleaded tearfully and with an anguished brow: "I can't stand it! Put it in my mouth! Please, please, please . . ."

He had, in the last few months, been to every cell on the tier and, for the most part, had been rebuffed. A few had accommodated him in these supplications of his to commit fellatio through the bars of the cells.

I was surprised, not at what he was doing to himself but that he had even called upon *me*. I become weary, actually drowsy —as if from boredom—when I am personally confronted with such things. Gerard was not a cocksucker, no matter what he thought of himself.

I must have shook my head slowly all the while he implored me. I know that at the point where his frenzy threatened to take complete control of him, I became impatient. I had to command him to stand up, to get off his knees.

I told him: "Get away from me! Go on! Leave!" He became sober and went away.

I knew him years ago; knew him when he was whole, when he was strong and dignified.

I look at him now and I search for that man I knew so long ago. Sometimes I catch a glimpse of the old Gerard and it is as if he were hoodwinking, saying: I'm just seeing what will happen if I do this; I'm only fooling everyone, to see who will stay loyal to me.

Gerard had a sly sense of humor *before* and it still shows itself once in a while. But he is not joking, not trying to fool anyone.

And it was not all that long ago that he was the Gerard I knew. Just a few years ago; no more than five. He is not insane, nor has his resistance to the prison regime ever flagged.

It almost seems as if he is rebelling against *us* now, although he will not attack any of us unless in self-defense. He'll fight us back as quickly as he will the pigs. I try to understand this madman who is not insane, but it is difficult.

Yet that look I catch in his eyes, the look I could take as evidence of deception, is something that makes me shudder. They say they see tombstones in his eyes.

In his writings Nietzsche speaks of the "glance of eternity," but I never paid much attention to the phrase, as if it were one of his magnificent poetic flights.

When I see Gerard's face, it jogs my memories and that phrase always bubbles up: the glance of eternity.

Free will—the will to personal power that recognizes no boundaries of either men or God—is shrouded with death.

Anyone could kill Gerard in retaliation and everyone else would protect his killer. Guard or prisoner. He is one of those people who tempt everything evil in men, and yet by *human* measure he is honest and his intent is never to harm.

It is as if the veil that protects us all from ourselves—as well as one another—had been pulled aside for Gerard so that he could see the actuality of everything. He cannot be deceived; you can hide no feeling or thought from him. He understands reality.

That is why he will someday be murdered—and he knows he cannot escape it.

I do not know how this change in him came about. It must have been gradual. I only know I noticed one day that he had gone to pieces. He used to clown around quite a bit. As I said, one of the things that marked him was his ability to laugh at everything; more often than not, himself.

He had been so often in and out of the hole, the guards placed him on the pay-him-no-mind list I spoke to you about. Can you imagine half a lifetime of prison regimentation? You are stopped by guards anywhere at any time and searched. Your cell is searched almost daily—and any little odd-or-end you happen to have, anything that is neither issued to all inmates nor explicitly allowed in a pathetic list of half a dozen items, is confiscated, and if it is in any way an object that *could* threaten security, you are thrown in the hole for it. You are stopped and questioned about the reasons for your presence in any area outside your cell. There are a million such things of this nature you are subject to daily.

Then suddenly, one day, it is as if you were a ghost. None of the guards can see you. You walk anywhere, and not only do the guards not stop you, no one *sees* you. I saw Gerard actually *climb* the inside perimeter fence and sit atop the rolls of concertina wire and wave to the guards in the gun-towers. He sat there for a half-hour and no one bothered him, until finally a couple of guards walked up to the fence and very politely and absurdly asked him to please come back down. He finally did, and they left him wandering around in confusion. They never threw him in the hole.

I believe men who take things seriously—take themselves more seriously than anything else—are the only ones who survive the pay-him-no-mind list. I have always grown dangerous and been taken off the list, although it has been tried with me many times.

. . .There have been times when I have begun the process of dissolution. The pigs can sense it and they pass the word. They place you on the *pay-him-no-mind* list. You are allowed to roam the prison and do and say *anything* you care to and the guards overlook it; ignore you as if you were not even there. Only if you commit an act of violence do they pounce and drag you to the hole.

The idea is to watch you and hope that in your state you will cause the other prisoners to dislike you, with the idea that one may kill you—or that you go on so long you lapse into that lumbering insanity which results from the derangement of your prison-senses. *Prison is abstracted from your sensuous existence.* You can do or say what you want. The place is handed over to you, in essence.

I used to stagger sometimes into the mess hall barefooted except for rubber shower-flops and none of the guards stopped me. I would walk around the prisoner queues and roam around in the kitchen behind the serving counters, picking up whatever I wanted to eat. The pigs would stand off, looking sideways at me and grinning. They would nudge one another in the ribs and wink.

I'd march out with a bowl of food in one hand and a loaf of bread in the other, in that crazy, directionless defiance on the approaches to insanity. I *insisted* on my freedom. I would march up the prison corridor to my cell like that, glaring at any pig who looked my way.

. . .Do you know what is so odd about this? I would be almost ready to kill myself. I wanted to be free so badly. *Always* I burned, truly *burned*, with the *need* to leave prison, to be *free:* to get away from this thing that was destroying my life irrevocably. I would sell my soul for freedom from prison, but I won't give an honest day's labor or "behave" myself for an instant for that same thing. Is that not strange? My poor soul! What a state it must be in to be bought so cheaply . . .

. . .It isn't prisoners who work out their petty relationships in prison. It's the prison system in America that drives them to outrages on one another. We are not to blame. We are not animals, but we are herded like animals. We are torn by the system of parole that rewards everything base and vile in a man. If we betray our poor comrades, we are rewarded. If we compete for the good graces of our jailers, we are rewarded. If we refuse to defend outselves, we are rewarded. If a man lets himself be used by the prison staff to catch another prisoner, he is rewarded. If he sucks your cock to get you to talk to him, he is rewarded for the information and congratulated for his method. There is no mistake made when prison staffs are regarded as brutal sadists who spend all their working time creating and influencing prison intrigues of the most vile sort.

They say that people who *live* together gradually begin to look alike. Married couples begin to "look" like one another because their facial expressions reflect an agreement about things around them, because their mannerisms and idiosyncrasies have become similar. They say it is a sign of genuine love —that the lover and the beloved grow into one. I have seen it. We all have. We all know it takes years of living together for lovers to become "look-alikes."

Something deep within me, however, turns over in its grave each time I notice that I look like my "brothers" who have been in prison all their lives. I have over the years *studied* the change in my appearance. It is the cast of an *outlaw*, an "outlander" (to use the archaic term). It is the face of men both *declassed* and *decultured*. Men who have become social outcasts, while existing in society, have this physiognomy. I loathe it, this lumpenproletarian cast of the criminal; this product of a war of nerves no one declared but which is forced upon us!

After ten or fifteen years, the sun never sets nor rises in a prison. There are no seasons: no wind or rain or sunlight in your hair. There are no children to give you a vision of life, no women to comfort your soul. I have never walked beneath the sky at nighttime on prison grounds.

Your needs are transformed into creatures that stalk you with reflections of every flaw in your personal existence. There is nothing so superfluous as the personal need to fulfill personal needs, and those needs become magnified and kaleidoscoped into such intense images and objects, they lose what little reality they had until you, yourself, are no longer *able* to accept reality as easily as you once may have.

You try only to keep yourself together because others—other prisoners—are with you. You don't comfort one another; you humor one another. You extend that confusion about this reality of one another by lying to one another. You can't stand the sight of each other and yet you are doomed to stand and face one another every moment of every day for years without end. You must bathe together, defecate and urinate together, eat and sleep together, talk together, work together.

The manifestation of the slightest flaw is world-shattering in its enormity. It is as if you very discreetly passed wind in a huge stadium and suddenly the thousands of people grow silent and look at you in condemnation. That is what prisoners do to each other.

GODS AND DRUGS

YOGIS STARVE their needs to death. I feed mine dreams. I put them asleep, but they always awaken again and try to move me about like a puppet on their strings. I am a white man, a civilized man, like you and all white men. The need to live close to God, the necessity, in other words, that breeds the certainty in our breasts that God exists, has been washed from our genes through history. Unlike you and most white men, my despair of God drives me from even the ritual conventions of religion, because, unlike others, I do not feel the necessity within me of social conventions that respect the dead. Unlike modern white men, philosophers, who despair of God, my despair does not drive me to the existential *act* of belief.

I do not believe in God, not because I do not want to but because *I cannot*. I do not believe in religious ethics because I cannot, and the same goes for all of my "beliefs." And for my "feelings." I cannot choose what I envy, hate, love or desire. If I believed the death penalty to be absolutely "immoral," I would not hesitate to save anyone from execution. Otherwise, my *conscience* would haunt me. Is all this a psychological aberration? Is it "idealism"? I do not think so. But I think all modern existentialist philosophy unconsciously aims at finding a way for a man to live with a guilty conscience, a conscience that haunts him. *Man* is a coward, plain and simple. He loves life too much. He fears others too much. And I would too, if I could, but I cannot live with a lie. But I have seen men who are such facile liars they can stick to their story for decades.

. . . It just occurred to me that any brand of theism must be rooted in some parallel brand of "faith." Displaced faith in society (mankind) and in personal beings *always* results in faith in some metaphysical world. Faith is a hell of a concept, a hell of a phenomenon. Existential faith for Sartre meant faith only in the distinction between one's ass and a hole in the ground (rather literally). For strange reasons too trite to go into here, he actually *said* that loss of faith (i.e., fear; phobia) in a *hole* (I mean that also *literally*) results (by displacement) in the phenomenon known as homosexuality. He really said that toward the last two hundred pages of *Being and Nothingness*. I read that thirteen years ago and still I have trouble believing anyone (even he) could be so crass, so stupid, as to say such a thing—even if it were, in a way, true. Idealists are so naïve when they talk about material reality.

. . . I find the human element in all religions very beautiful and touching. Religious ideas move me very much, almost as much as the people who hold those beliefs. I am moved by the knowledge that you find consolation in religious existentialism. I wish *I* could. You are a very lucky man. My readings of Kierkegaard, Buber and Jasper—to name three—left me inspired and changed me. What little emotional maturity I have I feel I owe to Sören Kierkegaard's works (after Nietzsche's childish ravings).

I want consolation more than anything in this world. I cannot help it if I have not been consoled by God, by a vision of the true Glory of God. I mean this with all my heart. Science is not consolation to me, any more than any abstract knowledge of the world can be a consolation.

The truth of religious existentialism is of a different nature than the truth of science. My problem is to live with both, because for some perverse reason, my life has been such that I cannot be happy, cannot be consoled, with just one of those. The two must be reconciled, and that is what Marxism has all the indication of possibly doing.

. . .*God, I need a fix now.* It is the only respite possible after so many years. Next month I begin working on my seventeenth year behind bars.

To feel the glow that begins like a fire in my belly and rises up through my nerves and organs, up to my temples, is something nothing else can give me. It gives me what I need to live with all this.

The other gods are nothing compared to this. You do not have to believe in anything. When it becomes necessary out of despair to believe in God, you have cheated oppression when you can live beside the beast without twisting your mind into believing it is God.

Someone said that if there was no God, men would invent one. The man who invented opium must have been the most rebellious. I believe the word, in this religious context, is *damned.*

Have you noticed how, in this hemisphere, drugs are tied into revolutionary matters somehow? This is true clear to the tip of South America.

I sometimes think it is our antidote to the devil. The "atmosphere" is so stifling in this the most powerful monolithic capitalist empire in the entire world. I do not "need" what the devil alone can give me if I have a few drugs (a little marijuana, mushroom, hash).

I wish revolution in this country were as simple as that in

industrially underdeveloped countries. I would otherwise end my life in the act of murdering a pig in the prison corridor. Especially nowadays, when prisons are so much "easier" (i.e., psychologically an inferno for an American communist). I would not last long without respites once in a while. These respites are only available through drugs.

Ole!

What if I am only justifying myself unconsciously with these words and they are silly excuses to be an asshole?

I realize, but not as fully as I should, that all these doubts about myself are only expressions of my isolation. Given the material freedom to act, to organize and develop situations and ties, no such self-doubt would enter my mind. I would laugh to remember these (present) days of my "reflections on my reflections"!

A comrade arrived here the other day from another prison. He thinks of discipline in terms of physical health (no smoking, no drugs, no punks, etc.). In terms of *calisthenics* almost. This attitude expresses an ultra-leftist tendency which has come 180 degrees; so far to the left, it is identical to the right.

He came to prison with a natural life sentence. This is his first time in prison. Although he has been in prison five or six years now, a lot of circumstances have, it seems, conspired to protect him from many of the realities of prison: other prisoners—and, therefore, himself.

He does not understand *vice*. He has the conscience of a bourgeois, i.e., he has an obviously bad conscience, which means *guilty feelings*.

He wants to stand aloof from the predicament of prisoners and yet he is one of them. Naturally, he has felt a few of their most pressing needs (to him very humiliating, shameful, disgraceful needs). He denies to *himself* he feels them and seems to enjoy denouncing anyone who does not deny such needs in himself.

He does not understand that men who are deprived of the

most basic forms of happiness will always find that happiness in other forms. Happiness is a serious need: a need as final, as inevitable, to the support of human life as sleep.

As long as he is a part of a people who can only find happiness in what people in other parts of the world call *vices*, he *must* feel the need for indulgence in those vices.

There are several escape routes out of it. There is insanity (I mean lumbering, slobbering insanity). There is suicide. There is co-existence, and by this I mean becoming a *tool* of those who govern us in prison.

None of these routes can get you away in one piece. All of them stem from fear of yourself, uncertainty about yourself.

I told him once: "You cannot as a communist revolutionary bring your spick-and-span ass into a Peruvian *bohio* and denounce the peasant-serfs for chewing the cocoa leaves for the cocaine and order them to first stop eating cocaine and wasting their bodies before they can organize for revolution."

It is one of the only forms of happiness *possible* for them. To demand such a thing is to demand they join forces with their oppressors, their patrons—who make the *same* demands.

. . .I started taking heroin a long time ago in prison. I had just knocked back three years in the hole, solitary confinement. I came out skin and bones, a nervous wreck (as usually occurs). My friends sent a kid to my cell for a present. He was excited about me and eager. I broke up the whole thing and sent him away and cooked up a fix. I used for emotional reasons, I guess. We all need emotional security. It's the only way I can get it, so I do it. It's practical and most convicts serving long sentences use heroin *for that purpose*. It is therapeutic.

. . .There is a kind of marijuana that is very good, very potent and expensive. It is the leaves of a sex-starved cannabis plant. A female cannabis plant is placed to grow among male plants, surrounded by male plants. Pins are inserted at various points of its stems to prevent the seeds from passing along the stalks to be fertilized by the males. She begins to quiver and suffer.

They say this plant, after several weeks, contorts in pain. They say at night, when the sun goes down, you can see it actually move. It pulls its leaves into itself as though wrapping its arms about its body for warmth. The idea of tragedy in plant life is created by man.

Everywhere I see suffering, I see someone who derives pleasure from the fruits of suffering.

. . .Some people get sloppy and ignorant; some go numb and dead; some get sly and paranoid—when they fuck with dope in prison. I get philosophical. I never realized this about myself until lately. When I'm alone in my cell floating in a narcotic wave, I begin to think about philosophical matters, and things have such clarity it is almost like the experience of satori.

Today, on hashish (behind Benzedrine), I kept a notebook by my bed and wrote whatever I felt important that occurred to me. It is fragmented but coherent.

I discovered there is only a *relative* difference between appearance and reality; the one is intrinsically of no more value than the other. I related this line to other things, and here are my notes, verbatim:

The interior can induce exterior change. *Vice versa:* We always seem to accept the appearance of things as being of less value than the "reality" of things. Why?

Men like me do not calculate value. This is why we fail to be stingy, fail to be properly clever in exchanging values with others.

Instead of calculating value, *determining its worth,* we instead refuse by a kind of built-in reflex to put a price on it. It then appears that we have no values ourselves, but in reality we have *no price.* There is a difference.

But as I said above, which is more "worthy" than the other?

Price and value. The one is no more "moral" or real than the other.

It is a vicious circle itself, something chasing its own tail in pursuit of something other.

After the abrogation of negation, there will be no contradiction between such things as "price and value." The things will exist but not the contradictions. How strange. It is a step higher in the evolution of our species; a step above the Homo sapiens. It is Marxism.

It is as though I were *weathering* everything in this world. Everything. Even my pleasures. Even when I am so happy I wish the moment could last forever, still I have an appetite to see it pass away. I weather even my greatest happiness.

The notion of spiritual existence in any form causes me anguish, despair. Marxism is my consolation.

It is this that common people sense in the doctrines of communism, Marxism. It is this they *identify* with the forces of Satan.

(A man with no apparent values who feels distress to the point of anguish over the idea of a spiritual existence.)

Men like me mean the death of god even before god is conceived. And we can make God perish from the world and everyone can also "sense" this in Marxism.

CHOOSING SIDES: COMMUNISTS AND MARXISM

THE BETTER part of my conscious life has over the years become deeply enmeshed in a political outlook. It is one of the inevitable products of suffering in prison—whether it is a "true" or "false" reflection is beside the point. It is me. It is all of us in my shoes.

. . .*Propaganda* is the truth told from a certain *viewpoint*. It defines the meaning of a thing from that viewpoint. It is not quite the same as *relative* judgment. When one says *one man's freedom fighter is another man's terrorist*, one understands what propaganda is.

The *opposite* of propaganda is *falsehood*. If I say something *occurred* that did not occur, I am *lying*. I am not engaging in propaganda.

When Christianity was still establishing itself in the Roman Catholic Church, there was an agency in the Vatican called

The Office of Propaganda. Its mission was to teach priests and Church officials how to interpret events from the point of view of the Christian religious doctrines. It was not established to propagate *lies*, but an *outlook* on the world.

Obviously, from a certain point of view, all the ills that befall men in prison are things prisoners bring upon themselves. This is *propaganda*.

From where I stand, no prisoner brings these ills upon himself—and one of the simplest reasons lies in the fact he is a *prisoner* and does not have the freedom to do anything to himself. But if *he did* have his *freedom*, one of the proofs he is free is that he will never injure himself, do violence to himself. This, too, is *propaganda*.

Whose point of view you side with and support is up to you.

I have seen what "blind justice" has done in all its horrors and I have seen physical torture beyond belief committed by prison authorities on prisoners. This is *all* bourgeois punishment.

The prisoners with the strongest *will* rebel. If they are intelligent enough to *read* and understand a little, they rehabilitate themselves *as men*, not through religion or prison regimentation or physical torture or "Thoughts on Capital Punishment," but through the comprehension of, and the discipline that attends, communism.

The government tells everyone that communism has to be taught through torture and that it imprisons and poisons men's minds, taking their "freedom of thought" away.

I assure you, until the left wing in society *pressured* the government, communist literature was *absolutely* forbidden in any prison population *here* in America.

I and others have risked serious disciplinary punishment obtaining and guarding communist literature.

. . .No one can (or ever has) accused me of not having a strong will. My I.Q. *jumped* from 127 to 138 over two years of intense study of the works of Marx and Lenin between 1966 and 1969. This was documented by a prison psychologist himself.

. . .If anyone wants to know why prisoners are so attracted to communist, subversive literature, the answer is simple: the communist press always tells the truth in reporting events in prison and in describing prison conditions. Is that so difficult to understand?

Prisoners come into contact with communists out of *need*. They do so only when they have no choice. They can write and appeal to senators, congressmen, civil rights attorneys, the news media, the courts—and on and on—all day long and not receive the slightest attention, seldom even a word of sympathy. And what are they complaining about? *Torture* at the hands of guards; *frame-ups for crimes* inside prison they never committed; lack of *medical attention;* capricious and arbitrary *discrimination;* the destruction of their mail; the interrogation of their friends and relatives outside prison—the list is not *endless* but it is long, longer than any list of grievances that prisoners in other countries can present. Communists give prisoners attorneys so that the courts cannot *so easily* make confetti out of their petitions in the clerks' offices. Communists inquire about prisoners and go into the streets among the people to stir up concern for prisoners. Communists conduct letterwriting campaigns to governments (state, city, federal, etc.), demanding an end to the maltreatment of prisoners. They do everything legally possible to help reform these prisons and to rescue prisoners from insanity, injury, death. They do this for *all* prisoners.

No one else does a thing. The liberals, the humanitarians and clergy are worse than anyone else. They are "too busy"; there is little they can do, etc. They stand around talking to one another about their experiences with prisoners; they seek to be "recognized" as *authorities* and "spokespersons" for prisoners. And never *once* have they ever as a group or as individuals effectuated a *single* reform or helped a single prisoner tortured in prison. Communists *use* them, their *names,* to accomplish behind the scenes prison reform. The FBI is correct in assuming this—but everyone denies it *out of vanity.*

Communists *always* behave as anyone would expect real people in a real society to respond to one another. *Communists,* not leftists.

If I had not come under their influence, I probably would have gotten out of prison long ago. But I would have returned, over and over again. I would have been a thief or a jive-talking dope fiend who has no idea of anything else in life except singing the blues and paying his dues in prison. Why? Because that is what the government, the state reared me from childhood to be; that is what adjusting to prison does to a man.

I am still very ignorant, but I can remake myself. My most important lesson is that I will betray anyone and anything in extreme situations. Everything except my beliefs, and I know mere "friendship," mere "blood," is but a sentiment. Anything, any tie I might have, that is based on a sentiment, is in danger of betrayal by me. I *never* do it easily; nothing is more painful to me than to betray a sentiment either in myself or others, and I've done it only once or twice in my life, but in my heart I have done it a million times. I consider it a weakness now to be loyal to any sentiment. In that way I am loyal to my heart, my "human weakness."

I have chosen sides, and in so doing I have won. I have learned to *always* choose sides and attack the other side as ruthlessly as possible.

Perhaps this is something a Castro could easily understand but a Sartre could never grasp.

When Dostoevsky pointed out that we are not generalized men, abstract men, the ideal "man," he did not mean to imply the opposite: that we are all ignoble, sensuous, weak, full of shit, etc. He meant that all of us, the ones "full of shit" (like myself), weak, sensuous, ignoble, etc., are *all* capable of dying for a just cause, a "beautiful idea," a *principle.* In short, that we are *all* capable of honor, not just the "Noble Classes."

He meant that the human heart is by no means a human weakness. Quite the contrary. Nothing that touches the human heart is absurd, because the Absurd is at bottom a contradiction and the heart chooses sides, defends a term, if you will, to the exclusion of the other. An insoluable contradiction is a *paradox*. A paradox titillates the human heart, does not burden it with despair of absurd, meaningless existence. Half the problem with Sartre and Camus and their ilk is that the bourgeoisie have forgotten how to laugh from the heart but not the belly. This is another thing a Castro can understand, but not a Sartre.

. . .When a man takes a position opposed to another and refuses to discuss the matter on the grounds that he feels that the truth of his position lies in a feeling in his heart that the next man does not have, he has taken an *anti-human* stand against humanity. This is because it is the aim of humanity to achieve a common *(social)* agreement. Any fool can see this is correct, since we are social beings.

In reality, only equals can reach agreements. So long as classes are not equal, men are not equal, and there is no way I can reach any agreements with the enemies of my class— particularly since these enemies hold the power of life or death over us. A man who "disagrees" that someone else should take his life is in no position to restrict this "disagreement" to words. If deeds will solve the "disagreement," they are as valid as words.

Sentiment is not the source of human weakness although today it is the tool of that weakness.

Some (Spinoza, for example) say: Love is that weakness, but when I speak of the human heart I speak of something imbued with love.

Today I think human weakness springs from social divisions. Today I think human weakness stems from the fact that human nature is still very much incomplete in its evolution.

In short, human weakness lies in the fact that no one is

perfect because no society is perfect. It is not the consciousness of this that pardons men from choosing sides. Only ignorance pardons.

Being conscious that no one is perfect is to intuit, to grasp with the heart the nature of an imperfection and to take a stand against it. This is called: *commitment.*

Dialectical Right contains Wrong. Anyone's heart can feel the truth of this. The human heart is betrayed if it does not maintain its integrity by siding against Wrong, by chasing it around the world if need be to stomp it into dust.

This is why Castro allowed prostitutes to organize (unionize their forces) instead of "abolishing" prostitution in Havana. He never let it go away and hide. Sartre did not properly understand this. This is why Lenin's party abolished *"laws"* (man-made), making sodomy a crime when the Bolsheviks took state power in Russia through the October Revolution. No law of mankind is just that abolishes men. The "higher" laws are the material principles that govern the universe as well as the societies of men, in spite of men. There would not be prostitution and sodomy if it were not necessary, and nine-tenths of the felt needs of men in a reactionary society are necessitated by unnatural conditions of social life.

Communists are closer to solving all the "riddles" of mankind than any scientists or philosophers in the past and present have ever been.

I do not mean to boast when I say this. It is not a "theory" but a *demonstrable* fact. I did not one day say: "Damn the whole world! I'm going to be *a communist!"*

Frankly, the word scared the shit out of me and I temporized a million ways, trying to evade this "infamous" title.

I pursued philosophy not as a disinterested scientist, not as a student or scholar, but because my life depended upon it. I was fighting to retrieve myself from my death throes. Who hasn't? Everyone has at some point in life. But my death throes lasted much longer; my life was much more endangered because I was fighting the *time* of my life and I have been in

prison a long, long time. Dissatisfaction with life itself drove
me, drove me farther than the rest.

I peaked with Hegel and Schopenhauer and regressed with
Nietzsche and Kierkegaard. But I advanced to a higher level
with Karl Marx and Friedrich Engels. Every advance in Marxism since then has taken me higher yet; Lenin, Stalin and Mao
teach the highest principles of human society.

Nietzsche felt the presence of communists when he wrote
of the philosophers of action, the philosophers of the future
who would come after him, such as Kierkegaard, who perceived
the death of faith and the birth of individual responsibility and
commitment. The thing-in-itself is knowable through *action*.

Marx put an end to philosophy, to philosophical studies as
we traditionally know them. He has given philosophers the
tools to change the world, and ipso facto called forth a new
kind of man who pursues philosophical problems.

. . .Essentially, Marx demonstrated philosophically that the
State was endowed with legitimacy not by God but by a ruling
class. In bourgeois society, whatever rights a citizen has are
granted by the State, by bourgeois interests. These rights support the existence not of the individual citizen but of the
bourgeoisie.

What good is one man to another in American society? He
is an object of exploitation. Whether what is sought are his
skills, his knowledge, his cooperation, his capital or his labor—
it makes no difference. Men imprison one another not just in
the concrete sense but in the most abstract and mental sense.
A man is originally an *obstacle* for men by the grace of those
very qualities which are sought in him. Ultimately, in this
society of men, it is Man himself who is an insurmountable
obstacle to men—and not Woman, who plays no decisive role.

The tragedy of the society of men is that it can never
dominate Man. Men can never be fulfilled as men, because

every advance in society drives men farther from themselves by the same measure that they require for themselves the qualities they must seek in other men. No man in American society has ever gone to his grave fulfilled, content, for this reason.

This is true because in his life he must confront, almost daily, a choice between good and evil and he must violate the good if he is to survive as a member of society. And what is meant by "good" if not the qualities of justice, equality, truth, freedom—all of those things we consider "ideals"?

How is this tragedy reconciled? How do men redeem themselves in their wholeness as Man? It is reconciled *in a farce*—and with no lack of poetic justice: all the romantic intrigues of courtship and consummation of sexual love between men and women in this society of men that *excludes* woman are *reproduced* in relationships between men. The powerful and wealthy magnate, the distinguished and honored senator, the ingenious and cultured scholar—as well as the common family man and the sportsman—find themselves one day, against their "holy" will power, infatuated with members of their own sex—the other man.

It does not matter if it is consummated, the *intrigue* remains. It can appear in the underlying competition for a woman; it can appear in almost every act of personal violence, especially in the psychological violence committed against the mind.

And in the history of all civilizations a *symptom* common to them all as they fall into flame and ruin is the image of that farcical fulfillment of Man embracing himself in passionate sexual love.

. . .I've spent a lifetime packed with others like sardines. The most *obvious* thing I notice is how easily people can be made to change. Fear and ignorance are the mental weaknesses that give access to people. The two are distinct; in *no way* are they identical. Words teach nothing but a vocabulary—in other words, words only address the imagination in one way or an-

other. The use they are put to should be to *act*, not to build
sand castles. People begin to really think and change for the
better *only* if they are forced *to experience things*, whether
good or evil. They become refined only in this manner.

If it were otherwise, life would hold no gusto, no surprises,
no interest. We would all be the same. Reform is merely words;
revolution is *action*.

A revolution is the most liberating experience, the most
glorifying experience anyone can have. It is a time when a new
world is coming into existence, when men and women carry
their own destinies in their hands.

. . .To me, to live is to change. That is fundamental to
Marxism. I'm not trying to convert you, I repeat. You are much
wiser than I. Wisdom to me is still a star in a galaxy light-years
away. You insult me by assuming I am so prejudiced I cannot
hold a conversation with anyone.

. . .They always say ineffectual, *effete* things. She spoke to
me as if I were part of a *conspiracy* and told me *"Violence
breeds violence"*—as if that was all there was to it.

I told her that revolutions happen outside the will of man.
That they are not conspiracies by experts. It does not matter
what anyone thinks about violence. They talk as though a
revolution is something that begins and ends with people taking "positions" on issues. A revolution is not a debating con-
test. No one "votes" for it.

The maxim which states *violence breeds violence* should
answer their own doubts about violence. If they think the
American government and its ruling classes and flunkies have
not *always* committed violence on the American lower classes
and weaker nationalities, they live in a dream all by themselves.
. . .There is nothing strange in the fact that a violent government, a violent class, *breeds* the violence that will someday
violently bring them to their knees.

. . .I understand the question that arises when they relate that it seems people can change for the better without violence, without experiencing the real force of circumstances of social revolution.

Aside from the fact that the experience of social revolution is a cherished wish of most of the world's masses—and *is not a dreadful thing at all*—I would concede perhaps it is a "bad experience" for the enemies of those masses.

The enemies—and they are mostly the political liberals and clergy—say that *"an awful lot of violence and anguish can take place simply within one person's skull."* I'm not used to talking like this, but this is one of the few cases where I can properly say such notions are "quaint."

God knows, I know all about "one person's skull"—but let me just say this. There are those who suffer from *themselves* and there are those who suffer from *others*. There is a *vast* difference. The first form of suffering is *illegitimate*. This by no means says it is not *genuine* suffering—the sufferings of a Hamlet. It is illegitimate because it really does *ignore* the suffering of others. Selfishness is a genuine form of suffering. Historically, it has always been a malady of the oppressing classes, the ruling classes. No one else suffers from it.

Words do not infuriate me. My beliefs are "arid?"—they *must* be because my *life* is arid. I have never qualified my belief in things like violence, and your friend ——— is indeed a "cultured Marxist"—nowhere near the Marxist I am—if he is unaware that Marxism-Leninism preaches violent conflict. If one phrase could characterize *Marxism in action in capitalist society*, it would be violent conflict. I do not like it and never said I did. But it is a fact of our society (and not, I believe, of "human behavior," as you suggested).

. . .The type of ridicule I like best is the eighteenth- and nineteenth-century "critiques," the *critical* method originated by Kant and refined in revolutionary writings. Marx was a master of it. To be able to breed contempt for something is associated with the ability to teach. You cannot teach by taking a thing lightly, by being airy about its surface—by *humor*. People *tolerate* things that amuse them, even if it doesn't "suit" them. But no one tolerates what he has contempt for. There are things in this world that need to be set straight. *Amusement* is not the way to get the job done; *contempt* is.

What creates amusement and humor is differences that *truly* are only transitory or *surface* differences. But to laugh at the differences between, say, the working class and the bourgeoisie *as if* they were only surface differences is to lie. The differences are *painfully* profound.

The anguish of a bourgeois over life (what tie to wear to the party) and the anguish of a proletarian over life (lack of shoes for the kids) are *not superficially* different. They are not equivalent.

. . .Once in the hole, serving about two years, I received letters from a fortyish woman who wrote me because some movement people asked the public to write and show concern, the idea being that if the Bureau of Prisons knew I had people outside who were concerned, it would save me from the goon squad after *every* meal, then at the psych building in Springfield. This strategy, all in all, did work. We became friends and I wrote a lot to her. I had nothing but my balls in that cell, but if I had a few dollars, I could have bought something from the prison store by ordering it. I had no toothpaste, let alone a cup of coffee or cigarettes. I once asked her (she was constantly ending her letters, *two a week*, with "Be sure and let me know if you need anything") if she could send me a few dollars and I *listed* the essential things I needed. She wrote me a haughty letter (I in a strip-cell, so fucked up even the sight of a piece of colored cloth moved me to euphoria), telling me I surprised her and that she did not like "materialists." She said she thought I was above "material things."

I quickly wrote her in my frenzy not to be abandoned, and apologized. She wrote me letters on rich, scented paper and sent them in scented envelopes, and told me about her problems getting into television acting and (I swear to God, I'm *not* lying) about her having "only one" *mink* coat that meant everything to her!

When you are so down that you will cling to anyone out there, you hit the bottom—or so it seems. There really is no "bottom"; it is bottomless, this pit of the "ten thousand things" that you fall through forever if you do not grab one of them, no matter how slimy.

I *am* intellectually consistent, stable. But when it comes to me, my situation, my subjective side, I can react to pain like a rattlesnake. No one likes to be hurt, to be injured, and all of this is painful. All of these things are mean, petty things anyone in any civilized society takes for granted but that I do not have. Anger, anger I'm not even conscious of, always burns within me.

And it is even painful to talk about it to you because you cannot possibly know this experience, for it is so close to my heart, the feeling is so *humiliating* and delicate, that it seems to me that one has to suffer through it to grasp what it really means.

It is as if someone rational and calm, someone on the gentle side, were to one day rage at you for what you take in essence to be nothing (perhaps slighted him accidentally in a minor way).

I know how it feels to be a *natural* ascetic, a *natural* Spartan, and to be comfortable in that asceticism, that Spartan outlook. And to have someone—who if she missed one meal would weep for pity—ridicule me for my "materialism," "selfishness," "scheming for things"—there is no greater insult to me than to be accused like that. And yet, as I said above, we all have to get a grip on something, no matter how little, to break the fall through that pit of the "ten thousand things" (I sound like a Chinese philosopher, I know, but I just started *The Secret of the Golden Flower* (by C. G. Jung and Richard Wilhelm).

. . .I can never be happy with the petty desires this bourgeois society has branded into my flesh, my sensuous being.

And what is so odd about it all is that society has denied me the *experience* it enjoys (or thinks it enjoys). The oddity exists in the fact that I *cannot* know from experience what I have missed, so why am I not happy?

I have been denied the society of *others:* it is as simple as that.

. . .You told me, finally, that I have a Marxist-Leninist vision and that those ideas die the hardest of all. Not really. It depends on who has those visions. You said you prefer "ideas which are fragile and delicate and have to survive each day and be re-created each day under the most difficult of conditions."

I think that perhaps you have scorned knowledge of "the most difficult of conditions" and are even now trying hard to scorn me and my condition. The most fragile and delicate of all ideas are those that reflect the fact that within human beings, there is an impenetrable area that *no one* can enter and defile: a heart of human tenderness so tenacious, so all-suffering and accepting, calm and *resilient to* human response, to love, that no force on earth can ever defeat it. It is the idea of the soul—and there are many of them; they are born "fragile and delicate and have to survive each day and be re-created each day under the most difficult of conditions."

I need beauty like I need to breathe. Do you imagine that those most cherished revelations, those ideas you speak of, do not come to me in that pit as they do to you? I know how transitory beauty is, but I also know from experience how eternal it is in the heart of man. It just now occurred to me that I would like to think I have captured some of that beauty for myself.

AMERICAN VIOLENCE/ AMERICAN JUSTICE:
The Legal System

I N AMERICA it has always been popular to follow mass murderers, crooks, killers of all stripe. America cultivates violence in everything it fashions, even people—the people fashioned by its vast, complicated governmental administration. *The Executioner's Song* should speak to America; should tell Americans that if the story of Gary Gilmore entertains them, if they thrill to the violence done to (as well as done by) Gilmore, then they should always be prepared, always have a gun or a cop within reach, because it will happen again and again as long as the American traditional system of violence stands above the use of reason.

For Americans to be shocked and disgusted at senseless murders and at crimes of extreme violence against the innocent is exactly identical to an old, worn-out prostitute expressing moral indignation at the thought of premarital sexual relations. Tell America that.

Tell America that as long as it permits the use of violence

in its institutions—in the whole vast administrative system traditional to this country—men and women will always indulge in violence, will always yearn to achieve the cultural mantle of this society based on swindle and violence.

When America can get angry because of the violence done to my life and the countless lives of men like me, then there will be an end to violence, but not before.

But whatever you say, tell America it is not (as Europe is fond of saying) a raging monster that was bred by the emigration of the worst blood of all the nations of the Old World. Tell America it is a cringing, back-stabbing coward because it cannot, has never tried to, exercise its will without violence. And because it is a coward, it does not respect reason. America resorts to the use of reason only as a *final* attempt to persuade, only after it has tried unsuccessfully to destroy a man, only after it is too late.

. . .The Americans who were ashamed yesterday of having served in the military in Vietnam are now saying: "I fought for my country." (!!!??) Are now *proud* of it. Proud of killing and torturing—mutilating—a doll-like people whose average adult male weighs under ninety pounds, stands under five feel tall, and tends to be a vegetarian and to practice that delicate form of sexual innocence called in the West "free love." Proud of deflowering a gentle and beautiful people!

. . . It is a big American pastime to talk about how horrible Soviet justice is—and yet America is *worse* than the Soviet Union! Particularly since no one in this goddamn country will help or gives a good goddamn what happens to us. *This* is the most unjust and oppressive country in the whole world, and I'm not going to go into lawyerlike details and comparisons. I'm not going to "argue my case" by their rules. I am totally convinced —and I do *not* believe I would have suffered greater injustices in *any* country in the world than I have here for a lifetime.

If I'm wrong, show me. That is what I have been saying for the last decade: *help us.* Bring justice to these courtrooms, jails, prisons.

. . .In prison, if I were asked the single most consistent cause of mental derangement in prisoners, I can tell you with utmost confidence: injustice.

First and foremost, the *injustice of the laws and courts of this land.* The injustice of the prison administration could be endured if that were the *only* injustice.

I can state as a maxim: Anyone in prison who has faith in retrieving the injustice done him by appealing to American jurisprudence will go mad unless he abandons it and *refuses* to ever believe there is an ounce of justice in any courtroom or prison in America. This *does not* apply to all countries. This I must emphasize. America is *far* from "universal"!!

If I have an *animal* whom I have taught to stand on its hind legs and beg on command, and it fails to do so, I must *punish* it in some manner to teach it to obey my command.

I inflict pain. I can do it by *deprivation* as well as with the whip. Any other way of teaching it to *always* obey would register in the animal as a *reward* for disobeying. This application of force can be humanely executed. I cannot *injure* the animal and still be humane.

If I commit force to a degree that it can be called violence, then I seek the destruction of the animal and not just the correction of a habit of disobedience.

So far, no one can dispute any of this.

I *taught* the animal to stand and beg by rewards. But if at some point or for whatever reason it does not properly obey and stand and beg, I may send it to an animal trainer. When I do that, I tell the trainer what it is the animal *knows* but does not do on command. I tell him to teach it to obey my command to stand and beg.

If I fail to do that, if I simply send the animal to a trainer to be trained generally speaking, the trainer may teach it everything but what it requires to obey the command to stand and beg.

The animal learns that any pain inflicted upon it by the being that nourishes and sustains it is pain it inflicts upon itself for disobedience. If it does not assimilate this "lesson" of self-inflicted pain, there is no recourse but the application of violence in order to *destroy* the animal. To kill it. It will *defend* itself with violence; it will become maddened and sullen. It will stand and fight or it will flee. It will do all this if it does not "learn" its pain is self-inflicted.

Do not ask me what all this has to do with American justice: it is *of the essence* to the American system of justice.

A prisoner begins his "training" in an American courtroom. He is told to shut his mouth unless spoken to. He is told he is a fool if he tries to be his own lawyer. He is told his motivations are not the subject matter of his indictment for crime.

His court-appointed lawyer tells him what law he violated and how many years in prison the punishment carries. He is told that if he informs on and betrays his friend, he will receive leniency. If he is the only one charged with the crime, he is told that if he helps solve other crimes, he could get leniency. He is told that because he knows the hour of the day and the day of the year and that he is in jail, he cannot claim to be insane. It does not matter that he cannot either read or write or understand the vocabulary or the rules of the court. It does not matter why he robbed a store—just that he robbed it.

If no violence was committed and he has a degree of wealth which places him above the need to rob a store, he will receive leniency in some form if this is his first indictment for crime. He *will not* be sent to prison.

Yet *he will* go to prison if he does not have the degree of wealth which places him above the commission of such a crime. He is sent to prison if he is poor. That is, if he is poor and refuses to (or cannot) act as an agent of the police to betray his friends and solve whatever crimes they committed.

If his lawyer likes him, he will dicker with the prosecutor and the judge to obtain as short a sentence to prison as he can. If his lawyer does not like him, he will not make that effort. In America today over eighty-five percent of all defendants who go to prison have pled guilty.

In all of this the prisoner never learns a single social value; never learns the definition of law or the customs of his society that the judicial system claims to be based upon.

Every right the prisoner has is turned against him. If he chooses to plead not guilty in order to receive a trial by jury, he will, if found guilty, receive the maximum penalty the law prescribes for putting everyone to trouble, for "wasting" everyone's time. His trial jury of peers is instructed *solely* to reach a determination of acquittal *only* if it cannot be proven by the government that the *physical event* did take place. The jury is told that his motivations are, in essence, irrelevant. The jury is *never* told it can acquit for any reason at all. The jury is *intimidated* into believing it itself would be in violation of the law if it did otherwise. Yet it can acquit out of nothing but personal sympathy. Not all the fine-honed, specious reasonings of lawyers and scholarly jurists in the world can refute this. It is a practical fact.

Men have pled guilty to murder and have been executed without anyone asking them the simple question: Why? In no other country on the face of this earth do such injustices exist today. There is no tyranny this profound in any country but America.

It is held in this country that the punishment *ends* upon sentencing and commitment to prison. This means a prisoner is not punished further, while he is in prison, for the crime. It would be "double jeopardy." This is what the law states—yet there are two black men who were sent to prison ten years ago as youngsters and the judge ordered that every Christmas Day the warden was to place them in solitary confinement until New Year's Day—and it is done. This is the spirit of American justice.

The prisoner enters prison. He is thrown into a violent whirlwind of moral, mental and physical destruction.

The government likes to boast that capital punishment is

virtually nonexistent any more. The government likes to boast that only two or three men out of over two hundred million citizens has been executed in the last twenty or twenty-five years.

Yet more prisoners are murdered today in American prisons than in any other on earth. About ten percent of America's prisoners are seriously wounded or murdered annually. Every single prisoner every day must exist with the *imminent* threat of assault at *the very least*—and from any quarter.

...The *sentence* to prison is the judicial punishment. A man is committed to prison for x number of years. So he sits in prison for x years and the law releases him. It is bearable because he can measure it, no matter how insufferable the prison conditions are. If he leaves an eye or hand behind, he is nevertheless getting out.

But when the judicial sentence is *indeterminate,* he is resentenced to a longer term every time any pig feels like it. Every time he is disciplined, punished for infractions of prison "rules"—which are as arbitrary as the currents of the wind— he is in effect *resentenced* to prison before the parole board.

There are no procedures before the parole board that guarantee him "judicial due process"—and this fancy legal term means no less than a *guarantee of justice*.

How does a prisoner count the time he must serve in prison when it has no end? If it was a life sentence, it still has an end. A prisoner can even face that he will die in prison—but by a happy chance may someday be freed before his life is over.

The mind's relationship to time is *fundamental.* What can the mind think when the fate of the man has been reduced to such a degree of uncertainty that he cannot predict the next day or the next hour?

The next day or the next hour could result in the certain annihilation of the (momentary) limit the law has supposedly placed on his imprisonment, his punishment.

He could break one of those petty, mean prison rules at any

moment and upset the balance completely. And also (more importantly) upset the balance of his mind. One of the greatest scientists and philosophers in the world said that the human mind is only conscious of a progression in time *because it can count* (Kant).

What happens when the mind experiences a progression of quantity it cannot count *in time*—for the reason that at any moment the mind must start all over again the process of counting because of events so capricious and arbitrary not even their uncertainty can be calculated?

. . .From here to there is five years. Each day closes the interval between my imprisonment and my freedom, which lies a moment beyond those five years.

At any point in that interval, I must stop and start counting all over again, over and over again.

For almost twenty years I have had to stop and start over many times. And I am *not* serving a life sentence. I have merely a nineteen-year *indeterminate* sentence—yet I have served, to this date, ten years of it. That is not all, however. I have now been in prison for eighteen years because before I started counting my federal time, I counted eight years in state prison.

But the parole board insists I have only been in prison for ten years. It refuses to "recognize" reality—because I have been free *once* since January 1963: I *escaped* once and lived six weeks as a fugitive before I was incarcerated again. Why have I served so much time? This is why: I do not recognize that I turned the key on *myself.* Others turned the key on me; I was sent to prison against my will and am held in prison against my will. What else is the meaning of these bars around my cage or those riflemen that keep constant vigil in the gun-towers that line the high walls that surround this cage? And they like to say that I am not perceiving *reality!*

I must face, or submit to mental derangement, that I must serve nineteen years to the day. I can therefore not "believe" the maddening promises that I, like all the others, will walk free before every day of my "indeterminate" sentence is over. The

only way a man can live with himself in hell is to abandon hope
—because prison in Christian society is nothing more than the
expression of Christian hell after death . . .

In the American judiciary, anyone who is sent to prison
suffers *civil death.* American legal scholars scoff at this today
and call it a thing of the past. If they would take their faces
out of their books and look a moment beyond official courtroom "facts" and events, they will find civil death is very much
in effect in every American prison.

How so? It is so simple any child can figure it out. There is
no legal *relationship* between prisoners and *any social* relationship among prisoners not monitored directly—a "forced" social relationship—by the pigs is in violation of rules. It is
insubordination.

No debt a prisoner contracts from another is not in violation
of rules. Serious rules. No prisoner can claim an obligation to
other prisoners without declaring war.

. . .There was once a prisoner named Blackie, and during a
riot he seized four guards hostage and held them through the
quelling of the uprising. In a battle with hundreds of armed
guards, one guard was stabbed to death and many hospitalized
for injuries.

It was one of those penitentiaries in which guards regularly
had fallen into the bad habit of attacking prisoners randomly.
No one ever went to the hole in those days without being
beaten as he was placed in a cell. One day the guards killed a
prisoner and there was a mass inmate uprising. That is how it
began.

Blackie took hostages in the middle of a pitched battle to
defend himself. He demanded the news media enter the prison
and hear the grievances of a committee composed of three men
of each race, and he demanded my release from the hole for
this purpose.

The national news media were not allowed inside the prison.
Instead, two local small-town newsmen were brought in. There
were nine of us, and we voiced our grievances until the morning hours and Blackie released the hostages unharmed.

He was later removed to a jail outside prison and no one ever saw him alive again. He was said to have hanged himself with his shirt from his bunk. For many reasons no one believed this. Blackie was well over six feet tall. He had been in prison seventeen years and loved life, especially his own.

He was not given an autopsy and the only witnesses of his death were guards. They in fact wrote the original death report.

A young intern came to see me during some legal proceedings in town and he spoke to me in hushed tones through the screening in the holding tank of the jail.

He had only *seen* Blackie's body at the morgue, but he told me that there was a crease an inch deep around Blackie's throat. The intern was specializing in forensic medicine and was an expert. He told me that over two hundred pounds of pressure had been applied to the noose and he explained the physics of it. Only two or three pounds of pressure is enough when a man hangs himself. His weight did not matter in any real sense.

The "law" states that prisoners cannot be buried without an autopsy at the least. But Blackie had no relatives. I tried to have him disinterred for an autopsy and filed a petition before the courts with the help of an attorney. The court, when it finally ruled, "recognized" that while Blackie was never given an autopsy, there was no living cause for action, since I was not his relative and had no legal claim on him. I tried to get around this by producing proof that Blackie was indebted to me, and his death had resulted in a legal financial loss the government must pay if it was found he died of causes other than suicide. The court ruled no prisoner can have obligations of any kind to other prisoners.

How am I going to get him out of his grave? How am I going to get justice for him?

As long as I am nothing but a ghost of the civil dead, I can do nothing . . .

The prison reform that took place for twenty years—from 1960 to 1980—never succeeded in establishing the constitutionality of *prisoners' rights*. It stopped short at the *civil rights* of individuals.

It has resulted today in consequences few of us dare to contemplate.

When the prison reform movement began, all a prisoner needed to do was send a letter to a judge and ask for help. The courts had the good sense to *presume* that there was a fundamental antagonism between a prisoner and those who held him in prison, and so the courts did not question a complaint outside the courtroom.

Today, the courts will not accept even a petition for a writ of habeas corpus unless a prisoner sends in a filing fee or a certified affidavit of pauperism—and the prison employee who is empowered to administer oaths is the one a penniless prisoner must turn to. He must get the cooperation of the prison in order to file a complaint against the prison.

In essence, the courts have returned not only to a "hands-off" doctrine in regard to *prisons*, but also in regard to any question that may lead to an issue of *prisoners' rights* (distinguished from individual constitutional civil rights). Therefore, the courts have even embraced a "hands-off" doctrine toward *prisoners*.

We have been handed over to policemen to be dealt with in any way it pleases them. I have never read or heard a true statement come out of the mouth of a policeman in regard to a prisoner's condition, and if anyone is curious about the mentality of policemen, all one has to do is have the vaguest notion of what a fascist is, a *political fascist*, and find out a few of a policeman's ideas about patriotism and democracy. The policemen are the law so far as a prisoner is concerned. The every whim of a backward pig is law for a prisoner today. A prisoner can be murdered, framed for crimes he never committed, tortured within an inch of his life—and all that is required in explanation is a single, unquestioned statement of a pig that there was no foul play on his part. Nothing more.

While in Leavenworth, a grand jury in K.C., Kansas, returned an indictment on me for a crime that carries a ten-year sentence: conveying a dangerous weapon. Do you know what it was? It was a *pen*—one of those long BIC pens. The little ball was missing, and so they decided I had altered it enough to make it a dangerous weapon in the hole. (Now, I have a copy of the indictment; if you disbelieve me, it would please me to send it to you. I was arraigned before a magistrate, and the BIC charge was dropped only after I was found "insane" on another charge.)

. . .The law has never punished anyone for hurting me. If I want justice to punish a wrong done me, it is entirely up to me.

Just picture yourself in that position right there in New York. You can't call a cop or the law when your house is burgled, when you are mugged downtown. The police walk into your home, slap you around (to put it mildly) and help themselves to whatever they want. Your wife and kids even. Anyone there in New York can accuse you of anything and you are punished without even knowing who your accuser is. You have absolutely no rights to legal protection by prosecution. The most you can do is file a civil complaint against the city. Hands are "slapped," but nothing is done. The "slapping of hands" is merely this. The judge says: "Now, Mayor (Warden), I hope this doesn't happen again." That's it. The mayor doesn't even bother to respond to the "admonition." He stands up, stretches, yawns and ambles away. All the faces around you, even the judge's, are covered with smirks. That's it. That's how I have had to live all my life.

What would you do? I assure you, you'd become a deranged coward or the exact opposite. If you become the former, everyone is happy and they'll give you little rewards. If you become the latter, they'll destroy you at every opportunity they get. They'll say you are "crazy," a psycho, etc. The "norm" is the coward in this situation.

To become *rehabilitated* means to accept and live by the values of your society. It requires not just faith in the laws and customs of your society, but faith in the people of your society —and to *extend* those values, and *reproduce* that faith, in your transactions with others in social intercourse.

To rehabilitate someone is a process of teaching. It is a process of *learning* by experience for the man in need of rehabilitation. He requires to know the benefits of the values of his society; he requires a firm understanding of the proper uses of the laws and customs of his society.

Only a man who is a social anomaly can fail to pursue his best interests, especially when the pathway becomes clear to him, for a social anomaly *knows* the values of his society and its laws and customs.

The system of justice in America teaches these lessons to men as if they were social anomalies *already*—as if they had *knowledge* of the values and customs and laws of this society. This reflects the American maxim: *Ignorance does not acquit.*

So rehabilitation is presumed and American justice seeks to *punish* men who (theoretically) know better.

And what does *punishment* that aims at *rehabilitation* entail? It does not aim at winning men over by reason—it is *presumed* a prisoner cannot be won over by reason. It is the application of force.

...A system of justice that does not instruct by *reason*, that does not rationally demonstrate to a man the error of his ways, accomplishes the opposite ends of justice: oppression.

No one in any prison in this country has ever been shown

the errors of his ways by the law. It is an annoyance no one in-volved in the administration of justice wants to be bothered with. So it is relegated to the prison regimes.

Everyone in prison has committed crimes, could be called a criminal. But that does not mean everyone in prison *belongs* there. I would like to suggest that there are men who are justly in prison but *do not belong* there. And there are men justly in prison who *do belong* there. Perhaps the great majority of prisoners belong there. They keep returning. I've seen them come and go; leave and return for so long, I've seen at least one entire prison turn over in population. Almost every one of them (in fact, *everyone* I've seen) feels relieved to be back. They need shaves and showers; they are gaunt, starved-looking when they come in from outside. *Within a week* they are rosy-cheeked, starched-and-pressed, talking to everyone. Laughing a lot (hail-fellow-well-met). They fit in in prison. This is where they belong. Or, to be more charitable—because if men pur-sue their best interests, no one really "belongs" in prison—let me say that there are less uncertainties in life in a prison than on the outside. It is not a matter so simple as that they have become institutionalized out of *habit*. That is not it. Prison is much more than a habit with men who belong here.

The point is: there are those—and they are not many, but they are men for whom prison does punish and punishes every day—who do not belong here in prison.

Let's leave off *where* it is they belong; that is not the point. They just do not fit in—do not belong—in prison. *I am speak-ing in terms of being, not justice or any other occasion.*

Luckily, those who do not belong seldom spend much time in prison and seldom return. But there are some who do spend a long, long time in prison. For them the hole was made.

Prisons certainly were not erected to serve the purpose of a boardinghouse; a private estate; a separate cultured commune. I submit to you that prisons can serve the purpose of rehabilitation of men. But there are men who cannot be rehabilitated, and these men belong in prison.

Society and not prison prevents their rehabilitation. For rehabilitation is something we *all* stand in need of; the rehabilitation of society itself has not been accomplished. This is reflected *also* in the fact that so many men in prison are not rehabilitated there (there in prison).

If society is so intolerable that a man can only feel himself to be a man in prison, it is the "fault" of society.

And I suggest that a few men are constantly rehabilitated in prison: they belong in society or they belong to be dead. But not in prison.

. . .No one has ever come out of prison a better man. I'm not talking about places like Allenwood and Maxwell Field—the places they send government informers and that frail species of individual who falls from the graces of the government or the Republican party or the Stock Exchange.

I'm speaking of the *penitentiary*. There is at least one in every state. Some states—like New York, Texas, California, Michigan, Illinois,—have at least a half dozen of them. The federal government itself has over forty prisons but only about a half-dozen penitentiaries.

I'm speaking *generally*. I do not mean to say anything "less" than San Quentin, Walpole, Leavenworth, Dannemora, Ramsey Farm (Huntsville), Anglola, Trenton—prisons of that caliber—do not fit into what I am saying here. They do.

For almost twenty years I have seen prisoners come and go. There is not *one* of them who comes to prison for the first time who is *capable* of the vast repertoire of crimes he is capable of when he finally gets out of prison. I'm not talking about the fine technicalities of, say, safe-cracking or the mechanics of murder. I'm not talking about methodologies.

No one learns those things in prison, contrary to the government's claims: prisoners do not learn how to commit crimes from other prisoners. They know how to commit crimes as well as you (reading this) do. Novels and the cinema teach more about how to commit successful crimes than anyone could *possibly* learn in prisons.

What is forced down their throats in spite of themselves is *the will* to commit crimes. It is the *capability* I am speaking of.

It used to be a pastime of mine to watch the change in men, to observe the blackening of their hearts. It takes place before your eyes. They enter prison more bewildered than afraid. Every step after that, the fear creeps into them. They are experiencing men and the administration of things no novels or the cinema—nor even the worst rumors about prison—can teach. No one is prepared for it. Even the pigs, when they first start to work in prison, are not prepared for it.

Everyone is afraid. It is not an emotional, psychological fear. It is a practical matter. If you do not threaten someone—at the very least—someone will threaten you. When you walk across the yard or down the tier to your cell, you stand out like a sore thumb if you do not appear either callously unconcerned or cold and ready to kill.

Many times you have to "prey" on someone, or you will be "preyed" on yourself. After so many years, *you are not bluffing.* No one is.

For want of a better expression, this is a *cynical experience* of life so *dangerous,* it changes you so that you don't even notice the change in yourself. In five or ten years, it's a way of life. You see pigs commit murder, and everyone from the warden on down are *active* accomplices. That is putting it mildly. The most well-known politicians and judges *actively* suppress evidence of such crimes. They are *rife.* You see it so often, it is routine.

It is routine to see guards make sure prisoners who have vowed to kill one another are forced into a cell together. Prisoners who have already demonstrated they will kill anyone. You see them kill each other like flies at the instigation and arrangement of guards.

The prison clergy, the easiest of all to intimidate, keep their mouths shut because (they whine) they cannot "prove" anything and, you know, the evil is outweighed by the "good" they can do if they just keep quiet and "do what they can." If they speak out, they are fired.

By the time you get out—*if* you get out—you are capable of *anything,* any crime at all.

Have you ever seen a man *despair* because he cannot bring himself to murder? I am not talking about murder in the heat of combat—that very seldom occurs in prison—I am speaking of cold-blooded premeditated murder. The only prisoners I have ever seen who do not suffer from that despair of being incapable of murder are those who *are* capable of it (not a few).

Most of them find—somewhere down the line—that they *are* capable of it. To discover that there was no basis for your anxieties about murder is a feeling similar to that of a young man who has doubts about being capable of consummating his first sexual encounter with a woman—and when the time comes, if he did not perform magnificently, at least he got the job done. You feel stronger.

If you can kill like that, you can do anything. All of the elements of every crime come into play. There is the deception; the ability to hold a secret; the calculation; the nerve—and the activity of well-planned and executed *violence.*

Most important, you learn never to trust a man, even if he seems honest and sincere. You learn how men deceive themselves and how impossible it is to help them without injuring yourself.

You know all of this and more in a conscious way before you get out of prison.

Why do you *steal* when you get out? Why do you commit crimes you never dreamed of being able to commit before you entered prison? You have changed so that you are not even aware there was a time you were incapable of such things. If you meditate on it, you tell yourself that you steal because you are no longer afraid of going to prison. This is because you do not remember you were not afraid originally.

The truth is that *money*—and I mean the wealth of a lifetime you have lost in prison—*cannot* be earned by honest labor. *Capital* is something that is expropriated: *stolen.*

All you require is a little self-confidence—and anyone who walks out of prison has that: he has confidence in himself, but no confidence at all in others.

The sorry thing about all this is that you truly did not learn how to steal properly in prison! The *very* thing the government and the apologists for American prisons charge prisoners with teaching one another. All the capability you have for crime never made you a whit more intelligent in that regard.

CAPITAL PUNISHMENT
AND GARY GILMORE

SOMEONE PASSED me a small book containing a selection of letters written by Marx. In it I found a fragment on *capital punishment.* This may amuse you.

It was an unfinished letter to the New York *Herald Tribune* in response to an editorial in *The Times* on capital punishment.

I found it interesting because Marx points out a causal relation within society between capital punishment and senseless, atrocious *murders and suicides.*

The Times editorial observed that whenever there was an execution—especially a well-publicized, famous execution—there seemed to follow "instances of death by hanging, either suicidal or accidental," within society.

Marx attacks this by saying *The Times,* with its hanging predilections and bloody logic, "has stopped before these phenomena at the *apotheosis of the hangman*"—in other words, that people were merely imitating the hangman. *The Times* ignored *the hanged man* as having any connection to these phenomena of "suicides and accidents."

Marx showed this by citing some data compiled by another newspaper (British), *The Morning Advertiser* (an enemy of capital punishment and *The Times*). The data cover a period of forty-three days of the year 1849, showing not only suicides but *"murders of the most atrocious kind, following closely upon the execution of criminals":*

EXECUTIONS OF		MURDERS AND SUICIDES	
Millan	March 20	Hannah Saddles	March 22
Petley	March 20	M.G. Newton	March 22
		J.G. Gleeson (four	
		Murders at Liverpool)	March 27
Smith	March 27	Murder and Suicide at	
		Leicester.	April 2
Howe.	March 31	Poisoning at Bath	April 7
		W. Bailey	April 8
		J.Wards murders his	
		mother.	April 13
Landish . . .	April 9	Yardley.	April 14
Sara Thomas.	May 9	Doxey, parricide	April 14
		J. Bailey kills his two	
		children and himself .	April 17
J. Griffiths . .	April 18	Chas. Overton	April 18
J. Rush. . . .	April 21	Danie Holmston	May 2

Marx merely acknowledged a relationship here, but he himself did not draw those parallels (or the table).

Marx points out that the bourgeoisie accurately predict the number and kind of crimes that will be committed over any given period, based on a number of approaches—including the above table. Budgets for prisons, scaffolds, judges (so on) are estimated on such figures.

Marx writes that it is difficult for the bourgeois mind to see *itself* as the *cause* of crime by creating the conditions legally.

Here the fragment trails off, but Marx coupled the cause connecting the data with the reason for compiling the data.

I would like to *add* that capital punishment was originally employed in law as a *punishment* for things we today view as misdemeanor crimes. A man was hanged for everything from pickpocketing to stealing morsels of food. It was originally effectuated to prevent petty crimes, *and not murder.*

In history, capital punishment appears *before* there appear the crimes of atrocious murders and suicides.

Not only do laws perpetrate the forms of crimes they "abolish," when they finally contradict the very *purpose* they were written for they *give birth* to other forms of crime. This is what has become of the death penalty in history.

Men like Son of Sam are consciously motivated by capital punishment. What else do you call their now-standard manner of toying with the police by leaving clues in the form of riddles and notes to mock the hangman?

That is how it can strike a morbid and immature mind, as Marx related in the fragment. But there is more.

. . .Here in prison the most respected and honored men *among us* are those who have killed other men, particularly other prisoners. It is not merely *fear,* but *respect.*

Everyone in prison has an ideal of violence, murder. Beneath all relationships between prisoners in prison is the ever-present fact of murder. It ultimately *defines* our relationship among ourselves.

And "murders and suicides" have not always been aberrant behavior in society. Before we reached this stage of civilization, our society had no such things as *murders and suicides.* The events these terms define today were not so defined then.

Ritual human sacrifice was no more a horror long ago in our society than capital punishment is to us today, and there are periods in our history when a man was given high honors only through acts of what we today call murders and suicides. A man who killed his father was looked upon with awe at one time, for example.

. . .I think that all people feel something special beneath the strata of social, everyday consciousness when they learn that one of their society has lost his life by an atrocious act of murder or suicide. It is as frightening to the common man, to the degree of frequency it occurs. It can drive him.

We are reminded that anyone in society can easily murder us, not just that anyone can easily be murdered. Death can come from any quarter where other people are present. In one degree or another, *we learn* this. It is not an "instinct": human expectation influences human chance.

The notion that capital punishment is a deterrent to murder contradicts itself before the whole world when someone is actually executed for an act of murder. It demonstrates *irrevocably* the opposite of the purpose for which the law was written: the men who are executed were obviously neither insane nor deterred in committing atrocious murder. The subject (the *hanged man*) has dominated the object (the *hangman*). The only way to prevail is to kill.

. . .The causal relation is the government, because it *connects* the death penalty with murder. Practical knowledge (common consciousness) does not distinguish the government itself that practices capital punishment with the apotheosis of the hangman.

. . .Your book about what happened to Gilmore should be accompanied by a little chorus of screams in the audience, don't you think?

If society punishes its members by death and imprisonment, why is anyone surprised when a *member* of society punishes his enemies with "death and imprisonment"? *(Que va! Savages!)*

. . . Everyone knows that America—that any modern, industrialized civilization—has the scientific means to alter a man's behavior. You can even call it "brainwashing," if you want to talk like a fool who has been sheltered all his life from the reality around us. We can "brainwash" a man so that he will not commit murder again. The whole world knows we can do this, almost effortlessly: *Do it humanely,* without destruction.

Why, then, does American society *execute* criminals? To execute a man in this country is perhaps ten times more costly than "brainwashing" him to never commit crime again.

It is *not* more "humane" to execute a man than to "brainwash" him when he has committed murder. It is not more humane to kill a man instead of making of him a *better man* who does not kill people.

This is the argument from civilization against the death penalty. It is anything but a *sophism*.

According to Marx: "Punishment in general has been defended as a means either of amelioration or of intimidating. *Now, what right have you to punish me for the amelioration or intimidation of others?* And besides, there is history—there is such a thing as statistics—which proves with the most complete evidence that since Cain, the world has been neither intimidated nor ameliorated by punishment.

The criminal is either a scapegoat or the *merchant* of his own soul.

This is the essence of the form of justice that we know today, in America in the last half of the twentieth century.

I say this is the *essential concept* of modern American justice and I don't want you to think I'm saying this is all there is to it. Everyone knows you can purchase our justice with one coin or another and that those denied "free will" by the circumstances of their class position (the stupid, friendless, poor, etc.) pay the price of the crimes of those more fortunate.

. . .I realize that I have completely identified myself with Gilmore. I assure you that there are many men like me; I am far from unique. We are not unique because we do not classify ourselves. Others do. In this case, the prison regimes, the authorities do. And if you went into any prison that held Gilmore and me and asked for all of the prisoners with certain backgrounds, both in and out of prison, backgrounds that include observed (and suspected) behavior, you will get a set of files, a list of names, and my file and name will always be handed you along with Gilmore's (and at least eight to ten others).

Gilmore appeared when convicts were principled, when being a convict was important. It was a time when a man was judged by himself, his own actions. Judged as an individual.

Then a transition began. Previously, if you were even seen in conversation with a pig, it could jeopardize your life. Shame on a snitch: he was killed casually, randomly. Now the prisons are made easy, because the pigs, I think, realize the value of keeping prisoners suspicious of one another and disunited.

. . .Nothing about his case is more easy for me to understand than his insistence on being executed.

To me, the problem of Gilmore is why did he kill a motel clerk and a service-station attendant in the act of armed robbery when they did not resist? It is difficult for me to grasp that.

You only reasonably kill like that if it is a robbery for a great sum of money. It is predicated on the motive that it will be your *last* robbery. Or you kill like that, if it is your *first* robbery and your *last* and you are desperate, driven.

He may have been a petty thief, an unsuccessful thief, but by his record alone you have to grant him a little expertise, a little professionalism. Anyone who has been in prison so long, so many times, acquires that gratis at the minimum (you might call it becoming "hip").

That is what deepens the problem Gilmore poses for me. What possessed him to do *that?* He could have at least driven to Salt Lake City to rob something, if he was worried about being identified. It is only thirty miles away from Provo.

I'm uncertain as to the nature of his intelligence. I do know he experimented quite cold-bloodedly with himself. (He once wore *half* a mustache; he steeled himself to do things ordinary men could not do; he was brave).

If he had the intelligence of men who are portrayed as "Nietzschean," he killed them for experimental reasons. Like Leopold and Loeb, for example. There was something in his intelligence that was morbid and sublime, from what little I can gather about him. Certain kinds of men incur the jealousy of the gods. But if God wished to destroy him, he would have first driven him mad. Even a communist knows that!

I do not understand why Gilmore did that. I want to understand, because then I would understand a little about what evil is.

. . .Sometimes (like now) I think Gilmore was one of the many "causes" that culminated in the deaths of those two men and that *they* are the real "effect." Sometimes I feel the focus of the "effect" should be on *them,* and Gilmore was but one of many causal forces that combined to effect their end, their deaths.

The problem here is just as great as the other: Where is the logical or existential *connection* between Gilmore as the cause of their deaths and the effect (their deaths)?

Thinking of it in such a way only leads up a blind alley and raises more questions than it solves.

I think a "cause-effect" continuum in this matter must be internal, primarily internal "movements." But to use this idea as an index to contemplate the matter throws open the gates to such a deluge of psychological and behavioral and ideological theories that you can hardly get a footing without reflecting your own internal private beliefs, because to say anything is to take a position among "schools of thought" and theoretical "systems" of thought, of belief.

But I know this. There is nothing as internal as pain, especially human pain. The catalog of suffering it would take to record the intricacies of pain that led to the manifestation of an act of multiple murder would be very melancholy to relate.

. . .However ignorant my impulses, I do tend toward philosophical matters. Sometimes I doubt that anyone with a philosophical turn of mind is fit to judge anyone. He never comprehends the concept of guilt.

That is not the concern of true justice.

The question is, rather, if he was privately guilty. For a variety of reasons he could only be guilty in his heart if he *chose* to be. Only he really knew. We can only guess at it.

His insistence on execution seems to point to that conclusion (among other things).

If I myself were certain and could *accept* his private guilt, knowledge of his prior innocence would itself acquit him in my mind, but I am not myself sure he should be privately guilty because of the kind of pain he must have suffered in his life, pain caused only by the consciously evil intentions of the penal institution in our present society.

It is hard to get at the truth of men. There are a lot of general "truths," but truth is always something specific. Still, I don't want to leave the impression that I feel at bottom man is vulgar, yet I'm sure you know I feel the opposite is true. At bottom men are principled; the vulgarities are acquired. When I say "principled," I in no way mean "innocent" or "full of love and good feelings." I mean, at bottom men do what they think and feel is "right"—whether good or evil. This means that at bottom men are not *weak* and I would never say, to justify a lapse in principle, "I am only human"—as though that were some kind of justification for weakness, moral weakness. Flesh and blood is much, much stronger than fools believe.

When Marx identified the "holy family" with men's dreams of paradise "on earth," he implied that the dreams would end should that paradise be realized. He implied that the conquest of the universe is the *sine qua non* of the conquest of man's dark side, of his instincts, of nothing less than the *unconscious*. Today one must begin not by studying the unconscious mind but by studying the world, the material world—a thing Freudians can't possibly understand. The universe obeys laws, a great variety of laws, but fools think this reflects that men are *not* born free and have no free will, when in fact this very belief enslaves men because only by knowing those laws, those principles, can men put them to use instead of being blindly tossed about at their mercy, the mercy of men's own ignorance.

So the pity of it is that neither Gilmore nor the world really knew what was happening to them. The level of civilization we have reached in this time and place was defined, illustrated.

. . .You said Gilmore wrote Nicole over fifteen hundred pages in three and a half months. I guess they reflected a lot of religious feelings. When one mixes poetry and philosophy, the result is mysticism, religion. It is emotional and impassioned "reasoning" before a fact we are all at the mercy of, we are all helpless before: death. I'd bet you could almost adduce the nature of his mystical beliefs from the nature of his particular death—from facts such as his formal, legal execution, his waiting alone in a cell for it, his wishing in the latter days to *will* it. This last fact is probably the most crucial to the unconscious formulation of his mystical beliefs: to create his own eschatology as well as his own afterlife, his eternity. *To will it.*

Only a convict, an old hand at suffering that special kind of anguish, could so absurdly wax upon the subject as though it were a conquest of his will when in reality he could not be more lost, could not be more enslaved.

You can't know how sad I feel when I realize the source of, and the nature of, the *involuntary* pride and exhilaration all convicts feel when they are chained up hand and foot as though they were vicious lions, dangerous animals. *They* make killers out of pussycats like that. It's as if suddenly we are in the spotlight, center stage. The world has focused on us for a moment. We are somebody capable of threatening the world in some way, no matter how small a way. That is why, for example, Son of Sam could not suppress that smile, that bashful smile pride causes in very humble, very *humiliated* men. Men in chains.

It is that involuntary pride of humiliated men that I feel was a strong component in Gilmore's emotions, his feelings, in his last days when the whole world seemed to be holding its breath to watch him die.

Nietzsche said things relevant to this in his *Zarathustra* in the verses of "Pale Criminal."

. . .I'm reading *The Red and the Black* again. It's been at least twenty years since I first read it. I can appreciate it more now that I'm older and from more points of view. This is one of the best portrayals of *romantic love*—the romantic outlook —that there is. It occurred to me in the first pages that, in this existential age, the last vestiges of romanticism appear to us today (in social intercourse) as *paranoia*.

Stendhal unwittingly presents Julien Sorel as a homosexual totally deluded from childhood into working out his desires on the stage of a society ruled by the male. The stage they walk about on and carry out their petty sublimations is woman herself. Stendhal, in this book, has succeeded in displaying people in personal relationships who completely misunderstood one another and yet continue together. I guess that misunderstanding itself defines clearly what the romantic period of our history was like.

Stendhal's women are really victims of men victimized by a (hilarious) sense of "duty," but one of them, Mademoiselle de la Mole, delivers a "biting epigram" she could have arrived at meditating on Gary Gilmore: "The only real distinction for a man is the death sentence." Not death itself, mind you, but the *death sentence*. I don't think the Mademoiselle, the daughter of a Marquis, knew men could be put to death without official sanction.

In other words, anyone who says Gilmore's real distinction was in his death sentence is involved in the "misunderstanding" I referred to above which I mentioned as a definition of romanticism. I'd like to know what Gilmore thought of himself there at the last. I can't help but to secretly wish that he was protected by some such delusion at the point of death. To be wrong is one thing, but to be so completely in error, so wrong that everything in existence scolds you for your mistake, is a terrible experience. I wouldn't wish it on anyone (except the bourgeoisie).

I've experienced it sufficiently myself not to wish it on anyone else. I think I will always feel the debt of apologizing for some of my mistakes. (To other people, of course. Certainly not the law!)

RACISM IN AMERICA
AND BEHIND BARS

FLIPPING THROUGH a booklet of excerpts from Marx and Engels this morning, I found, in a passage from Engels' *Anti-Dühring*, confirmation of what I said about the American policy of *human rights* employed as a political doctrine—a cry of self-defense, *exactly* like the plea of a prison guard held hostage at knife-point by a *prisoner* he has spent his working time *intentionally* tormenting: "But I have a wife and two children! Please, don't kill me!" *It is a ploy.*

Here it is:

. . . And it is significant of the specifically bourgeois character of those *human rights* that the American Constitution, the first to recognize the rights of man, in the same breath confirmed the slavery of the colored races then existing in America: class privileges were proscribed; race privileges sanctioned.

How is racism "significant of the specifically bourgeois character of those human rights"?

All of these human rights sanctioned the ideological doctrines of the Magna Carta, which established the *white man's right* (writ of habeas corpus), and Manifest Destiny, which established the *white man's burden* (colonialism).

Under the doctrine of Manifest Destiny, any white man could declare the sovereign rule of his land over any non-European lands under the auspices of various colonial mandates of the various white man's countries.

This is how human rights were established. They were established by *legal doctrines* which extend legislatively up to this very day.

The idea was that the white races would rule and administer the affairs of the non-white races; that the non-white races would become the source of labor and the white races would become the source of capital, i.e., civilization, wealth, culture. It is *still* in existence.

The race theory of humanity evolved in those early days of the bourgeois revolutions of the eighteenth century, but there was not in existence at that time the scientific tools required for proper scientific demonstration. Hegel, at that time, was the most systematic in his empirical "proofs" of white supremacy (cf. *Philosophy of History*).

The race theory of humanity states that the white races are the most advanced in the evolution of the human species; that the genetic structure of the white races is superior to the non-white races—indeed, it states that the darker the race, the more inferior it is to the "human race." The *human race* turns out to be the *white race*.

The scientific tools are the tools of *scientific empiricism*. Empirical observation and experimentation conclusively demonstrate the truth of the race theory of humanity. The so-called "humanists" take the position that the white races should guide the less fortunate through an evolutionary process to become—*white*.

This is possibly the "best-kept" secret in the bourgeois white world scientific community—and includes also twentieth-century bourgeois philosophers, especially in Continental Europe.

(Heidegger is one of the important "pioneers.") It is so "secret," few even *talk* about it to one another. I can imagine them in their white laboratory coats catching each other's eyes and arching a brow significantly every time some new data are gathered—or come in—that help to cinch "the theory"! *"The Great Experiment"* is drawing to a close! I can hear it now. (*The Great Experiment* is what, historically, the first bourgeois ideologists called *democracy*. Only later did it come to refer to the United States of America.)

The only statistics that "favor" the black masses of American society are those that demonstrate greater *athletic prowess* than the white masses. But this is even "explained away" by the citation of selective slave-breeding prior to the Civil War —and I have heard it explained away like this even by current black scholars themselves.

So there is no lack of empirical evidence to support the race theory of humanity. Crime statistics, social behavior, economic behavior, psychological response—the list includes everything. It is *because* of this list that this theory *culminates in genetic causes*—that is, according to scientific empiricism. It is already recognized in the athletic prowess of black people as an *inherited characteristic of race*.

Professor Shockley demonstrated that black people are *inherently* mentally inferior intellectually. He had the "bad taste" not to simply publish his finding but to talk about it, to *discuss* it in a "democratic society" of "free and equal" men. His "discussions" all *begin* with what is no longer for him or his listeners debatable: the genetic inferiority of black people. *What to do* about this is the object of his "discussions." The consequences to democracy are negative, to say the least.

The *only* scientific force in the industrial world that *opposes* —at least in theory—this race theory of humanity is the proletarian-class theory of history with the tools of scientific dialectical materialism.

Here is the *communist* theory in opposition to the capitalistic bourgeois theory (based on scientific empiricism):

(This is from the *Notes to Anti-Dühring* and it appears also in the appendix to Engel's *Dialectics of Nature*. It is from *Section (a) On the Prototypes of the Mathematical "Infinite" in the Real World.*)

. . . By recognizing the inheritance of acquired characters, it extends the subject of experience from the individual to the genus; the single individual that must have experienced is no longer necessary, its individual experience can be replaced to a certain extent by the results of the experiences of a number of its ancestors. If, for instance, among us the mathematical axioms seem *self-evident* to every eight-year-old child, and in no need of proof from experience, this is solely the result of "accumulated inheritance." It would be difficult to teach them by a proof to a Bushman or Australian Negro . . .

The accumulated experience of a number of ancestors—to use Engels' terminology—is twofold: the outward cultural traditions of a society, which includes books, tools, myths, etc.; and secondly, genealogically acquired experience.

Perception is based on these two areas of experience to become conscious knowledge. (Logic itself is one aspect of such knowledge.)

What is *self-evident* requires no proofs, for the simple reason it *cannot be placed in question* by someone for whom it is *self-evident.* And what is self-evident ultimately? The *world* is self-evident; the existence of the selfsame individual is self-evident. Those are the two things a Cartesian *could* not doubt so far as outward experience went for him. He could also not doubt the mathematical perception he entertained so magnificently. Descartes was a white man, a European.

Communist theory states that *prejudice* is an obstacle to *intelligence;* it states the bourgeois world outlook is a prejudice and that scientific empiricism is only the foundation of *bourgeois science* and not of science in general. It states that cultural and genealogical isolation is the *death* of all civilizations, and history has demonstrated this abundantly.

. . .It is a maxim that the morally strongest and the most

intelligent among an oppressed people are to be found on the scaffolds and in the prisons of the oppressors.

I have spent a lifetime in prisons with American Indians, Mexicans and Chicanos, and black Americans. Without question every non-white prisoner I have known is grappling with a revolutionary consciousness of the world—but the most consistent, the most persistent, are black prisoners. I have seen them so radical in their critical perception they cannot—*will not*—understand even a *paragraph* of conceptual language in a book. I learned early they *will not* learn by rote anything that addresses the everyday world. They will not clutter up their minds with (memorized) "knowledge" which is not *self-evident* to them. I have heard them point to the most abstract and seemingly universal "principles" and condescendingly say: "It is prejudice!"—and leave it there. I admit this was maddening to me, particularly since a certain amount of vehemence and hostility is always evident in their manner when they make such declarations.

Morons do not hold such opinions. Men with low intelligence do not become enraged over injustice; they question nothing and accept everything said and done to them.

. . .And whence came this "holy" white European Culture? It came as a *cultural inheritance* from the Roman and Islamic civilizations. European culture coalesced as a distinctive "entity" as a result of the ingathering of *many* races; many genealogical and cultural "entities." It began as an independent, specifically European culture roughly over the period we call the *Renaissance* (from the fourteenth to the seventeenth century). Islam and Rome had a similar history of an ingathering of many cultures, many races. The same is true of Ancient Greece and India and China. It is equally true of the Mayas and Aztecs in the Western Hemisphere.

Whether or not the world was round only became a question after it was no longer *self-evident* that it was square (or "flat"). Whether or not the world was the center of the revolutions of the universe—the "lights in the sky"—only became a question after it was no longer *self-evident* that it was so. The list of examples in European history is long.

Let me go with the world-is-flat example. It was once self-evident; no one in that culture doubted it. It had that *felt certainty* about it that forbade properly doubting it. From it flowed a whole world outlook, a whole body of knowledge. It had the *fixity of a popular prejudice*—and this is exactly what prejudice consists of. Anyone for whom that *fundamental* "fact" was not self-evident lacked intelligence and was considered a fool (in those days there were not any fine distinctions, such as idiot, moron, etc.).

Only a genealogically and culturally distinct people had the ability to be able to place in question the fundamental fact that the world was flat. Only those for whom it *was not self-evident* could do this. Only, therefore, the *fools* could do it!.

In a society for whom the world is flat—and *every* society is racially and culturally backward in this manner—all the knowledge of the world that contradicts the world being flat is erroneous: an example of ignorance or a mental defect.

In American (European) society the intelligence tests are not just *of* European culture, but are part of the European cultural traditions. These tests do nothing but demonstrate the extent prejudice has become a popular fixity.

People in European culture who have shined forth as true artistic creative geniuses are those who have been capable of *transcending* cultural prejudices, barriers. No academic intelligence test could possibly discover—except negatively, through the failure of the test—the high quality of this intelligence.

In *every* society in the world, the wisest men have always said, in one way or another, that only after they had pushed aside all they had learned as a student did they begin to exercise their intelligence.

. . .What is reflected in the European intelligence tests is, *overall,* a certain kind of self-evident knowledge called *mathematical.* Its *logic* is fundamentally mathematical. The *operations* of quantities and their relations (in formulations) are all self-evident. It is self-evident that if $A = B$ and $B = C$, $A = C$.

The intelligence quotient is itself a way of mathematically judging the degree of fixity (in the popular mind) of the self-evident axioms of mathematics. *Nothing more.* It means that the most passive and obsequious—ultimately ignorant and dependent—people in our society will score the *highest.*

There is no such thing as a "de-cultured" intelligence test. Even if the mathematical method is employed and the quotient is a ratio between the *genetic* age of a certain people (in substitution for the chronological age of an individual) and the *cultural* age of that people (in substitution for the mental age of that individual), still the quantity of positive and negative ("true" and "false") answers *creates* a mathematical judgment of values of qualities—values that are *not* quantitatively measurable.

Machines can calculate. Therefore, calculation is the *lowest* form of intelligence.

Whatever must be learned by rote is a *prejudice;* it is not knowledge. Knowledge is something that has a subjective side, an intimate meaning as well as an outward meaning. The tune of the hickory stick across the butt of a schoolboy is not the proper *experience* required to inform his intelligence—and any goddamned fool should know that. All he is taught is what a dog is taught: *to obey.* He is not taught to *understand* what it is he is doing when he obeys—even saying his obedience is based on "love and kindness"—unless the fool who is whipping him thinks that x number of *thumps* across the butt is what the arithmatical number x is composed of.

But this is the *best* illustration: In actuality (for I suspect x number of thumps just may be what the number x is composed of!), the boy is being taught (e.g., *whipped*) what *concepts* are, what *things* are, more often than what mathematics is.

He is being *whipped* what history is; what ideals like justice, equality, etc., are; what passion and poetry are. The boy is being punished in order to learn—a poem! Punished to "know" what is true, good, beautiful. A truly gifted boy would *turn* on his "teacher"—And what? If he had a pistol, he would *shoot* his way out of school the way Carl Panzram did. That is what he would do. Then he would probably rob a bank and get out of town—fast!

This is what made the "Chinaman of Königsberg" (Kant) say: "Genius makes its own rules." Even European philosophers have taken notice that most of what we take for knowledge is nothing but bias and prejudice.

The point Engels made was that we would not demonstrate to "a Bushman or Australian Negro" what is self-evident to us —but that a Bushman or Australian Negro *could,* because he (and not us) is in a *position* to do so for the simple reason it is for him *not self-evident.*

Nor can humanity(!) look upon itself the way it does other species of life. "Humanity" may "know" what the best strains of wheat or cattle or dogs are, but only in relation to itself (at best). It can breed strains of life to bring out certain qualities it seeks in a species, but it *cannot* breed scientifically the qualities that make up a *human being* (a complete, many-sided human being). This is not because humanity cannot breed people; it is because "humanity" is in no position to know what a complete human being is. At present we know what we once took to be human traits are actually cultured and genealogical peculiarities. We know that as a species we are still evolving, and to arrest that growth would be to arrest our evolution.

. . .I'm surrounded by Mexican aliens here. No one speaks English. I speak a little Spanish. Some of them piss in the shower and refuse to flush toilet tissue down the toilet—you see heaps of shit-stained toilet tissue go past your cell in the wake of the trustee's pushbroom when he sweeps the corridor. Flies move in herds, like miniature cattle grazing a few feet above the floor. The Mexican border is only two miles away.

In Mexico—as in most foreign countries—the water pressure in sewer plumbing is too low to accommodate the flushing of wet paper through the pipes. This is why most of them who have never lived in this country—and speak no English—do not flush the toilet tissue down the toilet.

A racist could make a big deal out of this. Do you see the relationship between ignorance and prejudice?

. . .I wasn't always in prison! Hell, I was free once. I was free for about five months—maybe five and a half months—in 1962. (I'm a *man of the world!*)

I have *seen* racism outside prison. I do not like injustice. Some people do; that is why I have to state that I do not. Here are some experiences I had before I went to prison:

In the summer of 1962, before I was sent to prison, I went to Texas. I arrived in ———, Texas, by bus. At the bus station there were two identical drinking fountains. One said White Only and the other said Colored Only. It was the first time I remember seeing anything like this. I thought it *funny.*

It was in July of 1962 and the civil rights movement in the South was over with. What I mean is: before the large participation of students in the anti-war movement joined it.

The sizable cities of Texas all had their Colored Districts, but in the small towns in the country, there were no Colored Districts.

Blacks could not enter those small towns without a "legitimate excuse." After dark, blacks caught inside the towns risked death.

The small town my folks lived in—my grandparents—was named ———.

In the small towns in the country, instead of a Colored District, each had what they called a *nigger-town!* It was as though they were shadows of the real towns. They seem to reflect *in concept* the psychoanalytic relationships between the conscious and subconscious mind.

In the town of ——— blacks came in from *nigger-town* when the sun rose. They washed the windows of the businesses; swept the streets and sidewalks and picked up the garbage.

Then they left town before the stores opened. I was at a movie house—the only one in town—and I rose in the middle of the movie to go to the restrooms. Walking up the aisle, I happened to notice in the balcony that all the seats were occupied by black people. I discovered they were not allowed to sit anywhere but in the balcony. I believe they had to purchase their tickets for the movies at a certain time each week. They could not merely walk up to the ticket seller at movie time, like white folks do.

I took most of this racial discrimination to be only an eccentricity of the South. I never attempted to guess at its implications.

Then one day I was watching the news on television. There was an on-the-spot news flash covering an event there in town. I switched off the television and left the house. The news event was happening about a block away.

A black man as big as a house was at bay against a wall of the bus station. He was a farmer from the town's *nigger-town*. He must have been successful at farming, because he had a big International-make hauling truck filled with neat bales of hay. He had a little boy, about nine years old. The boy stayed in the cab of the truck.

The farmer's truck was double-parked over one of the white lines that separated the parking spaces. But there were no other vehicles parked there. He had come into town to purchase a block of ice. The bus station, which sat on the outskirts of town, also had an icehouse.

A cop had fined the black farmer two hundred dollars, with the alternative—if he did not pay instantly—of being hauled off to jail. The farmer did not have that much cash in his pocket and so the cop tried to arrest him. The cop called for reinforcements and about eight or nine more cops arrived.

One tried to grab the farmer, who pushed him aside. There was, at the edge of the parking lot, what remained of a barbed-wire fence. All that remained were cedar posts sticking up from the ground, and the farmer jerked a post out of the ground and backed up against the wall, brandishing the club in one hand. He had to have been strong as an ox, because cedar posts are always buried deeply.

When I arrived the cops had him surrounded in a semicircle, with, as I said, his back to the wall.

Every cop had his pistol drawn and aimed at him. They shouted at me to stay back, but I walked up anyway. Before I reached the police, they opened fire on the farmer. I froze, because I could not believe what I was seeing.

The farmer was merely standing there with the club raised. He did not attack. I heard him shout over and over: *"Leave me be!"*

They emptied their guns in his body. He jerked each time a bullet hit him. They were shooting him with .44-caliber ammunition—more lethal than .357-magnum bullets. They were firing at him from a distance of about twenty feet. He was dead before he hit the ground.

The little boy was wailing, watching his daddy die. I saw that his truck was parked so that the front tire of the truck, on the driver's side, was over the white dividing line about six or eight inches. The talk later circulated that he was one of those "crazy niggers."

When I left Texas by Greyhound bus, there was one other incident that struck me. These buses are engaged in interstate commerce and have no regulations once aboard the bus that discriminate as to race.

I took a seat by the window, in the middle of the bus. All the seats were full except about seven or eight seats on the aisle. A black student about twenty years old boarded the bus. He was the only black there.

I was lost in thought and staring out the window when he stopped and inquired if he could sit in the empty seat next to me. Absently I said: "Sure, it doesn't matter." He sat down. I still was not conscious of anything special. We spoke a few words idly. He had boarded with at least one other college student, a white boy from Idaho.

When the bus stopped at a café for supper, we all got off the bus and entered the café. The black student and I sat together at the counter. I remember vaguely asking him where the other student had "disappeared" to. Then we both ordered supper from a waitress.

In due time mine arrived. *I began eating.* He inquired about his order to the waitress. *I kept eating.* He inquired about his order to the waitress. *I was through eating.* He inquired about his order again, and by now I was getting impatient. She told him that his supper was in a brown paper bag "to go."

I looked from him to the waitress, still so innocent I did not understand what was going on—but it was clear they did not like one another.

I was so stupid I thought that his supper-to-go was because the bus was going to depart before he could finish eating it.

He took the bag and paid his check. He and I walked outside the café. There were fifteen or twenty passengers standing about on the sidewalk and along the bus. White folks.

He stepped onto the lawn and I followed him. He sat there on the grass and opened his bag while we talked. We talked about nothing that had anything to do with the situation—at least I thought so. But I recall now that he kept asking me carefully, between bites of food, where I was from. I kept telling him I was born in Michigan. He would chew his food and nod and blink his eyes.

The old ladies, the old men and all the others watched us closely. I remember that they all grinned at us in a very engaging manner. We were the only ones on the lawn. I thought that amused them.

I kept looking in the crowd for the other student, the white boy. I caught glimpses of him, but he apparently never saw or heard me when I would call to him. Every time I glimpsed him, his head was in the act of turning.

When we boarded the bus again, the black student said: "I ought to picket this place." Then we resumed our seats.

That was the first time it dawned on me that blacks were not allowed to eat in the café. We were still within the Texas border.

I recall the better part of our conversations was about cities in the United States. He told me he liked San Francisco. At that point the white student spoke up. You know how they do it: catching my eyes intently, he addressed the black student and observed that I could get rich there. "How so?" I asked, curious. The white student giggled, and the black cleared it all up: "Hustling," he said. Then he leaned forward toward me and said quietly: "The dude is a fag—know what I mean?"

I guess the only other experience I had in racial discrimination of black people that left an impression on me before I went to prison occurred in Salt Lake City.

There was a big dancing place owned and operated by the Mormons. It sat right on the edge of what was then a black neighborhood. It was Second East Street on the corner of, I believe, Seventh South Street.

The place was called Liberty Wells.

No blacks, Mexicans or Indians allowed. The only things visible there were the white faces of physically healthy and even attractive young white people in their late teens or early twenties. They all had the slow mentality of cattle, the evil intelligence of one of those elderly virgins of the Victorian period who teach schoolchildren the alphabet and to properly hate themselves.

It was about ten or eleven o'clock in the evening and I was walking through the area. I stopped at the curb, waiting for the traffic to pass. Liberty Wells, I noticed, was having a dance. It sat kitty-corner from where I had paused. Six or seven blacks about my age walked up and waited with me for the traffic to pass.

I crossed the street with them and continued down the sidewalk, directly across the street from Liberty Wells.

There were thick oak trees along the sidewalk on one side and a chain-link fence on the other side. There was no light at that point.

The blacks crowded around me and I stopped. The largest one stood in front of me. The first thing I thought was that I should have carried my gun. I told him to get out of my way and started toward him. He said: "First you have to fight one of us."

Then he pushed a scared smaller one in front of me. I brushed him aside and stepped into the spokesman. I hit him with a right and went for him, ignoring the blows from all sides. I got my licks in on him before I hit the ground. I rolled to the fence, and all I could do was lie there and try to block the kicks.

While they were hitting me, one kept yelling something about not being able to dance. Then they ran down the sidewalk. I stood up and brushed off my clothes. About twenty whites were gathered at the foot of the steps leading into the dance hall, watching.

I looked at them and it made sense. I continued on my way.

Today I realize I have had to pay the price many times for the social injustices committed by white people in this society. I have never been close to them, have never had much in common with them. And by that I mean white people who are in a position to commit these racial injustices. I had never been to a dance at Liberty Wells, nor ever cared to.

Getting attacked by blacks is supposed to turn me against them. It is supposed to force me into the ranks of white society.

It is a form of "rehabilitation"—and in many prison systems, it is virtually the main rehabilitation program there.

It has worked overall, I would say. There you will find prisoners who are attracted to racial doctrines, but not near as many as the policemen in Los Angeles and Orange County, however. It has never been lost on me that beneath the robes of the Klan, you are more than likely to find a policeman. Indeed, it was Mussolini himself who justified his "revolution" of policemen by saying that "the working people will be happy only when there is a policeman on every street corner."

Excuse me, but I could never support the police!

When I think of the *profundity* of the injustices done to black people in America, I feel a horror I cannot easily describe.

I would not be a man if I believed that blacks are not *justified socially* in treating any and all white people in this society with violence and hatred. Even as I write this I am aware of white boys being raped and murdered in prisons, of white men and women being attacked and murdered by blacks.

There is such a thing as social justice—it is not a question of *individual* justice. White society created black society through racial discrimination. (The phrase "racial discrimination" seems to be light-years removed from the deep horror white society gave birth to, and nurtured: *the nigger.*)

The peculiar way the bourgeois class in America developed brought this about. I refuse to sanitize it by offering yet another "class analysis" of the history of racial oppression in America. Just the same, there is a class basis for it.

It is not in the *nature* of "white society"—or white cultures —to oppress other peoples.

There is no democracy for blacks—for all non-white Americans—in this country. America is a white man's country, and this is not simply a result of blind economic laws.

I was once reading some old booklets that contained minutes of the U.S. Congress at the turn of this century, and there was a debate concerning the need for legislation to control foreign emigration to America.

A quota system based on race alone resulted from this. The senators were concerned with stemming the tide of Chinese and Japanese immigrants.

I can quote exactly the principle for determining the quotas: *"If America is going to remain a white man's country,"* said the senator—he was not a famous senator and I have forgotten his name—*"it is our duty to restrict entrance into this country of non-European races."*

A quota system for *all* immigrants was worked out and enacted by Congress to insure that far more white people than non-white were allowed into the country.

I remember when the State Prison was racially integrated for black prisoners. It is incredible to recall today. There were exactly six blacks out of about eight hundred prisoners. Segregation of so few seems absurd beyond belief today, yet in the history of the state—over a hundred years—black prisoners had been segregated. The Chicanos and Indians represented almost half of the prison population and were never segregated. When this happened—and it happened all over the country —it began a struggle for the rights of *all* prisoners. When the Civil Rights Act came into existence a few years later, it permitted prisoners to enter federal courts and sue for their rights to be free from discrimination and cruel and unusual punishment. It began a period of prison reform that had a revolutionary effect on prison conditions for the vast majority of all prisoners.

We no longer had to fear being tortured and thrown into the hole for writing a letter to a judge, a lawyer or a senator. For the most part it became possible to communicate with anyone through the Postal Service. *Playboy* magazine was no longer a contraband item punishable by twenty-nine days in the hole on the "starvation diet." We had a right, for the first time, to medical care, to proper food and clothing. We had a right not to be loaned out on shotgun crews for slave labor to private businessmen. The screen barriers were torn down and for the first time we could touch and kiss our people in the visiting room. They unchained me from the floor and quit tear-gassing me in my sleep. It became unconstitutional to use electroshock therapy to punish prisoners.

The list is endless.

It is true that when these things came into being, more "sophisticated" and subtle forms of abuse arose. It arose in the form of prisoner killing prisoner.

Until then, there was a harmony among prisoners. There was a line that divided prisoners from the prison staff and it was understood by us all. We were once one. We were united not just in our misery, but as men; as men regardless of race.

There was violence and murder between prisoners who crossed that line as informers—not because a man was "black" or "white."

But it was nothing to the violence among prisoners that exists today. And this violence can be measured by the number of caseworkers, psychologists, sociologists; by the number of prison employees who are not ordinary prison guards. It has come about in typically freakish America that prisons do not merely try to reform thieves—their goal, conscious or unconscious, is to make *policemen* out of prisoners. The same way government makes policemen out of criminals and drug addicts, who are turned into informers outside prison.

Society, which has never in reality accepted blacks as equals, gives them "equality" *only* in prison, where they immediately exploit that equality to get back in prison what society outside prison deprives them of: power.

The problem of racism is politically disturbing to me. I believe I have grappled with it in political theory all my life. I see a blind injustice of such towering proportions, it is difficult to take in all its ramifications.

Oppressed races and nationalities in prisons *immediately* seek to assert the kind of supremacy over whites that whites subject them to outside prison. It is almost a mechanical law —and "should be." It is the only time and place in this country most non-whites can redeem the promise of their childhoods, namely, to be men.

In most of my letters in this regard, I mistakenly had before my eyes the ideal of *individual* justice—and it was, all along, a matter of social justice.

. . .Justice is not always bloodless and it does not always visit the individual. It is above intellectual considerations and it draws its morality from consequences.

. . .The word "nigger" is itself offensive, I have come to realize, in spite of attempts by both black and white anti-racist intellectuals to use it in a non-derogatory way: to defuse it. Nothing can redeem that word. When blacks call one another "nigger," they have *accepted* that they are inferior as human beings. It is the same when homosexuals call one another "bitches"—they have accepted that they are inferior as men.

. . .It has been something I have been aware of since I started serving time: So long as, and to the degree that a prison regime can keep its prisoner at each other's throats—to that degree can it abuse and torment its prisoners; to that degree are the injustices of American prisoners multiplied. In the South the prison regimes use mainly *a class* of prisoners who behave as guards, pigs. They are called variously (depending upon which state) dog-boys, building tenders, convict guards, trustees; the list is colorful, and every state in the South has its own name for these inmates. They are given *all* the authority of regular prison guards. They are even armed with rifles.

Out in the Western states, prisoners are divided by race. In some cases, the prison regime will give privileges to blacks and Chicanos and Indians which they deny to whites. In other cases, it is whites they give all the privileges to. They implement this in many ways. They can use inmate organizations called "culture groups." These groups are given resources not available to others of races not of a certain "cultural group." (Outside visitors on a social level; "freedom"; etc.) Another way is by harassing *only* one race—more times than not, *today* it is the *white* prisoners who are the ones being tortured and discriminated against.

At Leavenworth and Atlanta, I was always thrown into all-black cells, especially in lock-up if those prisons held up to four men per cell. Outside lock-up there are eight-men cells. I was always the only white man there. The idea was to get me attacked by blacks. The idea was to get me to hate blacks.

I personally have never had any problems with them, either in lock-up or on the yard. This is because I am known among them. But my case is exceptional, and as a rule whites are turned into active racists by this method.

They have always placed the most outspoken black Muslims in cells with me in lock-up, but I have never had any problems.

This is because we share a common oppression: at bottom, class oppression and racial oppression are identical. Before I even knew what the word was, I was once told by an old black man when I first started serving time that I was *class-conscious*. (I looked it up in my books to discover what it was.)

. . .Every *leap* in the direction of prison reform is preceded in prison by a period of racial unity among *all* prisoners. Work strikes come about quickly in quick succession; prisoners fight back against beatings and are supported by everyone on the yard. Sabotage on the yard—at work sites—follows quickly upon any prisoner tortured in the hole.

A period in which pigs address prisoners decently is accompanied by prisoner unity.

. . .We were packed in cells in the hole immediately following the riot. A black prisoner was taken out and severely beaten. His jaw was broken. We dumped on the pigs, tore up everything we could. This was in the largest of the federal prisons. The pigs were afraid to let us shower for fear we would attack when they opened a cell door.

About three weeks later they let us shower one at a time. About twenty pigs escorted us, one at a time, in and out of the shower stall from the cells.

They were all white pigs and they stood directly in front of the shower watching me and trying to act relaxed. One named *Punchy* said, in a friendly voice: "We're white men like you. Those blacks don't like you any more than they like us." He watched me and I just said: "Fuck your mother."

If the pigs would approach *me* like that, I know they must do it to other white prisoners. It makes me wonder sometimes when I look at the faces of prisoners around me.

We were sent to prison *to be broken*. The forces that arrested us, gave us "due process" and threw us into prison, hate our guts and wish to heaven we did not exist. It is not an accident that we all too often find ourselves in racial conflicts of self-defense with other prisoners.

They want us to kill one another. So long as we are murdering one another, we are making it easy for the prison regimes and the police to hold us and destroy us.

If I offered here the figures of prisoners killed and wounded in prisons and jails in the last decade or so in America, you could more easily understand that an armed conflict—a war, even though a "small war"—is taking place at this very moment in every state, every county and in every city. It is being orchestrated by the police at this moment.

Every day of every year in America at least four prisoners suffer violent death in prison and over one hundred are wounded.

They use the blacks against the Chicanos, the whites and the Puerto Ricans. And the whites against the Chicanos and the Indians and the blacks and Puerto Ricans. They use every race against every other race, and that is why they are not tearing down the prisons.

Prison regimes and jails "teach" white prisoners to hate non-white prisoners, because after being socially subjected to white racism all their lives, the blacks naturally attack white prisoners in jail and prison.

The authorities want the white prisoners to change their ways and "come back into the fold of white law-abiding society." That's the message and it is as clear as a bell.

Whites are *forced* to defend themselves in prison, even if part of that defense is to take the offensive position. American prisons are not Sunday schools.

Whites have to stay close to one another in most of the large penitentiaries and defend each other. This will be true so long as it is not understood by all races of prisoners that it is to their advantage to live in harmony and mutual regard for one another. Until then, mutual destruction will be their lot.

But this can never happen. The police, the prison regimes will always see to arranging our lives in prison with an eye to keeping us at each other's throats.

FOREIGN AFFAIRS

THE COMMUNISTS who *led* the peasant (and petty bourgeois) revolutions in 1848 in Germany failed for *political* reasons. The communists had not devised a correct political policy for winning the peasant classes over to the proletarian revolution gathering strength in the cities of Cologne, Paris and London.

The lessons derived from Marx's analyses of the communist experience in France and Germany furnished the basis of the *Leninist* Communist Party, which called for a *worker-peasant class alliance—an alliance* that permits the proletariat, small in number in peasant countries, to rule the government.

The first successful revolution *led* by the communist proletariat occurred in 1917 in Russia. Since then, the whole history of the development of nations has *shifted.* The proletarian movement since 1917 has gathered such immense strength throughout the world that a world proletarian revolution is not far off. The revolution depends on the worker-peasant alliance and its ability to maintain its *independence* (economic and political) from the bourgeois industrial nations—concentrated for the most part in Europe, specifically: England.

Every *peasant* nation that frees itself by an alliance with the Communist Party, the *dictatorship of the proletariat,* from the imperialist monopoly capitalism of other nations, brings us closer to the hour of the successful proletarian revolution that is spearheading, historically, the world revolution.

What happens in Mexico, Central America and South America, in Africa and the Middle East—in Third World nations—will *determine* that hour, which *is* inevitable. It could take ten more years, it could take thirty or a hundred more years—but it will come: It is inevitable.

What role the communist superpowers will play in this is another matter. China and the Soviet Union could possibly *retard* the world revolution. I am not certain as to their *place* in the communist movement today. They certainly have no claim to leadership (and *are not* the *vanguard*), simply because they are vast and powerful. Little Albania or Mozambique, for the sake of illustration *only,* could possibly play a more important role in the movement *(in every sense)* than the big, powerful *communistic* countries like the People's Republic of China and the Soviet Union.

The role of these superpowers will depend in an *absolute* sense on the *assistance* they extend to the revolutionaries fighting for their lives in the Third World now, *today.* These revolutionaries are being *tempered* in a revolutionary *war* for power and are, therefore, in possession of a higher revolutionary consciousness.

I am with the most feeble and oppressed of all the Third World nations. I direct my concern there. I hope to be in England when the first successful proletarian revolution occurs . . .

There are perhaps many reasons why I seem to "admire" Russia, but the main one is this: I have developed a feeling that responds to the Russian soul—the greatest writers of prose came from Russia. I see Russia as a great suffering mass of humanity that has wallowed so deeply in the mire that only great passions could result.

Besides, I first studied Lenin and then all his comrades. I studied the history of the Communist Party he led. The "old guard" of Russia and all of Europe during Lenin's time are vivid presences in my mind. The personalities of Lenin and all his comrades impressed me. I feel I know personally Liebknecht, Luxemburg, Kautsky, Radek, Bukharin, etc., etc. I can even imagine what it must have felt like to win a country with my comrades and nurse it to health. To see the realization of years of theorizing, of dreaming. To walk with comrades in patched-up suits from every corner of Europe and America across a country we just conquered and to feel the might that is at last ours.

. . .I have read at least three books by Alexander Solzhenitsyn: *August 1814, The First Circle* and *The Gulag Archipelago*. I have also read a few articles by him.

He is a traitor, not to communism (you must first have been a communist), but to his people, his countrymen. (Notice how America is a haven for the vilest of traitors!)

I was delighted to read *The First Circle* because beneath all his shit, I learned a lot about how lenient the Soviet Union was to its prisoners. I have been in prison twice as long as he, and I am not a traitor who tried to hand his country over to another country. He served ten years in prison for a crime that would most certainly result in execution today in the U.S.A. If not execution, he would still just be starting his natural life term in Leavenworth. In either case, he would never in his life have been freed. I have served more time than he did, just in the hole.

He was/is a *militarist,* one who worshipped *German* militarism. He is not even a propagandist: *he is a liar.* He tells his lies, weaves his fabrications, with a certain amount of *style.* The style of one committed. A certain passion. That passion is simply to lie his way out of a bad situation—and he has exulted in it!

. . .It just occurred to me this morning that you see in my disgust with Soviet "dissidents" (like Anatoly Shcharansky), *a pro-Soviet attitude.*

There is a movement—and this movement, ironically, was born in the Soviet felon prisons—to restore communism, Marxism-Leninism, in the Soviet Union. I support it.

There is a petty-bourgeois movement in the U.S.S.R. to establish *complete* bourgeois freedom. I oppose it. The "dissidents." To me, the "dissidents" are ridiculous. Not only are they ridiculous, but I find in them a cynical verification of the maleducated "intellectuals" the Soviet Union is producing.

. . .My position regarding Cuba and Cuba's relation to social imperialism is this: historical developments have conspired to force Cuba (if "appearances" are correct) to kneel before the U.S.S.R.—to be a "running dog" of social imperialism. First of all, Cuba is *alone* in the Western Hemisphere. Cuba had either to capitulate to America and restore conditions prior to the Cuban revolution, or align itself with the "communist empire" of the Soviet Union.

I do not agree with Cuba's foreign policy because *Cuba has no foreign policy.* Cuba has the foreign policy of the Soviet Union.

The only way Cuba can break with social imperialism is if two or three Latin-American countries have a successful revolution. This would break Cuba's isolation; give her a voice in the Western Hemisphere and allow her to form, if necessary, some sort of bloc to punish her enemies. That was Che's conception of Cuba in relation to other hemispheric powers.

I cannot be critical of an infant whose only possible source of nourishment can be found in the dugs of a wolf.

Lenin made his Brest Treaty. Stalin his Pact with Hitler. Lenin saw the Brest Treaty as a means of gaining time, a means of respite. Stalin saw his pact as necessary, which indeed it was, because the Western Powers wanted to pit Hitler against Russia and then move in and defeat whichever side emerged victorious.

Lenin's treaty and Stalin's pact were politically brilliant maneuvers. Their response to reality was magnificent. So is Castro's.

Mao, the Chinese Communist Party and the country are objectively three separate entities.

I support Mao's influence on the revolution, his contribution to Marxist knowledge.

I support an independent China.

I do not know enough about the C.C.P. to judge whether I "support" the party.

Under Mao, China had a military like none we ever heard of. It did not have the best "weapons," nor did it rely on weaponry. But it had the best *people* because they were politically trained, and this element alone defies everything we once knew (or know) about regular positional warfare.

I think this is the crux of the difference between bourgeois military doctrines and the military doctrines of people's war. The former relies on weaponry and machinery; the latter on the valor of the people. The latter is vastly superior in war. No one seriously contests this any longer—not at the Pentagon; nowhere. The greatest innovation in warfare in the twentieth century is not the discovery of nuclear war—it is the discovery of people's war.

The capitalist military can never use the methods of people's war without *overthrowing* itself.

. . .The thinking is that the Jews in the U.S.S.R. who want to go to Israel want to get there for the express reason of picking up *arms* against the Palestinians. That is why a lot of people have reservations about the mass Jewish migration from the U.S.S.R. to Israel. That is *not* my "automatic" opinion. I don't *hold* that

opinion, because I honestly do not know. I have no opinion
except, of course, that if Jews want to go there to live with the
same motives anyone migrates to another country, it would be a
crime to stop them. But there are rumors to the contrary, and *I
do* know what Zionism is, as opposed to Judaism.

. . .I wince when I hear that life in Israel is like life here in
the U.S.A. If that is supposed to be a kind of defense of Israel,
it only tells me how corrupt, how evil and terrible that country
is.

If you do not understand the devastating nature of civilized
violence—violence that makes the horrible atrocities of savage
violence look like childish play-acting—you have not truly com-
prehended the setting for both my letters and the contents of
them. That violence that destroys a man's character, his morals, his life, his mind and perverts all of his senses is the violence
that stalks beneath the banners of capitalism and settles like a
plague over industrial democratic republics.

The Shah of Iran will chop off your hands, but he will not
(because he *cannot*) take your soul from you. In America, for
example, if its prisons hold the slightest authority over you, it
both can and *will* destroy you—it can and will take *your soul.*

We are each of us here burnt-out disaster zones—the more
pitiable because most of us don't know it or can't see it.

I am not "for" either *civilized* or *savage* violence. Civilized
violence is, however, the worst of the two. It is a compulsion
without personal reason that permeates every aspect of life in
bourgeois society. Marx called it "alienation."

So for me to visualize an Israel "like the U.S.A." is for me
to feel alarm; to feel life is infinitely worse there in quality than,
say, even in Saudi Arabia or Syria—with its barbarian monarchies and savage tribes.

. . .I wish you would ponder this a moment. Say that all the
Arab nations tomorrow became *partners* with Israel and every-

thing that implies. The feudal monarchies would be supported by all the interests that support the existence of Israel. The inevitable collapse of those old feudal systems would be held at bay for God knows how many decades.

Revolution would be stifled. We *need* instability in that area of the world in order to raise up the people in that area. All the Arab nations are beginning to become aware of this. We need to raise popular democratic revolutions in all the Arab nations now, and communists are trying to do just that.

This "great country" has sure become *enraged* with righteous indignation over the Ayatollah's latest farce to get a little justice out of the U.S.A. by forcing the extradition of one of the most infamous war criminals since the Second World War. Imagine how the Israelis would react if the U.S.A. not only harbored Adolf Hitler, but *feted* him, made him an honored guest. No one argues that point, of course! It is the "methods" of the Iranians they take "issue" with.

Go out into the streets. Ask anyone: from the man on the street to the "experts" in political science at Harvard and Yale. See how red their faces get, how angry! At last, *at long last,* their "country" has been done an "injustice." They are *up in arms* against the Iranian *children* in this country for daring to show solidarity with their revolution—a revolution that has been historically overdue for forty years; a revolution that is barely in its infancy: six months old. It *needs justice.* That means that the Shah *cannot* walk free in the same world as the people of Iran. A friend of an enemy is an enemy. Childish but true.

The old yellow pus of American cowardice is once again throbbing in the veins of this sorry country. How does it appear? In chauvinism that struts safely in its own land, away from danger. It is easy to talk "dangerously" about knocking people down when you are on your own turf, behind an embattlement of thousands of nuclear missiles and an ocean.

This shit revolts me to no end if I don't think of something else. If I dwelled on it, I just know I'd tear up this cell in rage.

FREEDOM?

LIGHTNING is flashing outside the windows and a torrent of rain has come. It is about midnight and everyone is quiet. They always are during a hunger strike. It is my time to stretch out and relax.

This kind of night—the rain hitting the windows hard, driving—has always soothed me. The roll of thunder sounds like the big drums of a symphony orchestra.

When it occurs to me the kind of things it takes to make me happy after all these years, I like to think they are simple. Simple because money cannot purchase them. Indeed, money is an *obstacle* to them. But I know I ask too much. Then again, it's not a matter of what I like or dislike, what I "want" or desire. Not a matter of personal taste. It is what I *need*, what my existence cannot live without. Some would call it "revenge"; others, "vindication." I want justice.

I do not want to be in prison so long that I come to gaze up at the sky and curse the stars for my misery. I do not want ever to come to the upside-down conclusion that "no one is to blame," as the saying goes. Or that this state of affairs always has been and always will be in our world. Or that I turned the key on myself.

. . .I do not know how I would react to the experience of someone, an ordinary man who works for a government, who would come up to me and with his manner, his tone, his *voice* tell me: "We apologize for what we did to you. We are sorry and will never do it again."

If he were truly sincere and I *knew* it, such an experience would devastate me. I believe it *would* alter me radically.

I might as well forget that. It is not unlike the man who says: "I'll believe in God only if I see Him." In reality his secret desire is to believe, and he *does* by presupposing God in order to *"see"* Him. But he never *"sees"* Him and is never reconciled to his beliefs by an objective but *personal* act of God: only by his own acts.

. . .The main thing too obvious for me now to overlook is that it is *constitutionally* impossible for me to exist in prison.

My vision of life outside prison has become a fading dream. It makes me wonder if that is what it has always been all along. I think I want out of prison the way the average man thinks he wants to be a millionaire, or to be, which is a better example, a great artist like Michelangelo. Not having the faintest notion of the sacrifices and effort that such things require in the average man.

Counterposed to "my vision of life outside prison" is my full-blown perception of a terrible revolutionary war in its infancy—flaring up in fits and starts and dying as quickly in a splash of blood and violence on a scale so microscopic as to go unnoticed to the average, everyday perception of events in this country. The realization that by all odds I too will be just one of those unnoticed "fits and starts" that dies terribly in a splash of blood and inhuman violence, indifferent violence, is not very heartening. Nevertheless, the line of my life leads inexorably in that direction. That vision has conquered the pastoral one of life: the "normal" life.

The first "natural" revolutionaries ever born to society always die in prisons, always die after long torture and debasement. They are always unknown, unsupported, and usually unconscious of themselves as such. They think they die as "good thieves," "good convicts."

The Catechism of a Revolutionary, written by Natcheyev, describes such men. But it describes their Being and not their direct consciousness as revolutionary. Every detail of our society is my annihilation. It has been since my birth. The morals, customs, laws of our society oppose my existence in essence.

So maybe this explains a little of why it seems that I do not "really" care whether or not I am ever released from prison. Simply to die a violent death on a "bigger scale," (a bigger "splash of blood") instead of in prison, can be itself reason to exist with the desire to get out of prison (the "little scale"; the "little splash of blood"). History understands only big things.

. . .I cannot imagine how I can be happy in American society. After all this that society has done, I am naturally resentful. I don't want revenge; to punish. I just would like an apology of some sort. A little consideration. Just a small recognition by society of the injustice that has been done to me, not to mention others like me.

Am I to be content to walk free along the same streets as men who have entered my cell and beaten me to the floor, with full knowledge and consent of everyone? Men who have come to work and spent their working time tormenting me?

Or walk the streets with the scores of judges, of politicians, preachers and lawyers who have consciously conspired to crush me through the perpetration of intentional *lies*, cover-ups? Who have baited their traps for me with my very sanity? With justice? With common decency?

Or walk the streets with the "faceless masses" of our society who during my lifetime have supported or acquiesced to evil men and their ambitions? And do it with full cynical knowledge?

Just *you* walk out of your house and stop one randomly on the street. Talk to him. It may amuse you because he has never had power over you. You are not subjected to his ignorance, his basic evilness.

But if you had been, you would not find it amusing. I have been all my life under his arbitrary heel.

How I wish this would end! How I wish I could walk free in the world, could find my life again and see and do things other people do.

I don't see how that would be possible now, though. Too much has happened, for too long, to me. But I want to try. It is my right. *That* is what "human right" is. *My* right, the *individual's* right. We all have that right even though we know in our hearts we may be incapable of accomplishing what we have the *absolute* right to try to accomplish. If society has the right to do to me what it has done (and is still doing), which society *does* have, then I have the right, at least, to walk free at some time in my life even if the odds are by now overwhelming that I may not be as other men.

. . .I do not know how I feel at being given a parole. The thought of legally being free from prison receded from my mind, my feelings, so long ago that I honestly do not recall a time I ever had plans or hopes of ever being a free man in this country again in my life. Maybe later I can write about it, but not now.

INDEX

ABOUT THE AUTHOR

JACK HENRY ABBOTT was born January 21, 1944, in Oscoda, Michigan. He has written for *The New York Review of Books*.